DECISIONS, DECISIONS: Style in Writing

DECISIONS, DECISIONS:
Style in Writing

Mary E. Whitten

North Texas State University

HARCOURT BRACE JOVANOVICH, INC.
New York   Chicago   San Francisco   Atlanta

Part Opening photos and cover photo by A. Grigaitis, DPI

ISBN: 0–15–517260–3

Library of Congress Catalog Card Number: 75–141612

Printed in the United States of America

Preface

Every writer makes decisions. He decides what to say, what not to say, when to say what, and why. He decides upon a type of composition, a method of developing each paragraph. He decides whether to use one structure or another, one word or another, or both or neither, whether to use one mark of punctuation or another. The English language provides many alternatives, and different writers make different decisions. It is these differences in choice that make differences in style.

Style has to do with how a writer chooses to say something. Whether a style is clumsy or graceful, childish or mature, ineffectual or dynamic is determined by these choices. As Wilson Follett has observed: "The formation of any style, even a bad one, is an affair of constant acceptances and rejections; and everyone has to lean on his own taste for acceptance of the better and rejection of the worse." When accepting or rejecting, the writer has at his command a wide range of possible alternatives.

And alternatives are what this book is all about: it presents a wide range of decisions that writers make. When converting one sentence pattern to another in Part 1, or when analyzing and imitating paragraph models in Part 2 or essay models in Part 3, students may become familiar with new structures and discover new methods of expression. Some students may for the first time consciously observe the differences between structures, between types of paragraphs, between kinds of compositions. Every student who uses this book may gain new insight and a fresh understanding of the importance of choice and its relevance to an effective style.

Gerald Levin of the University of Akron and Henry W. Rink of Foothill College offered valuable criticisms as well as many helpful, practical suggestions. I also wish to thank Miss Audrey Ann Welch of Denton, Texas, who as critic and writer made an important contribution to this book.

Mary E. Whitten

Contents

Alternate
Structures

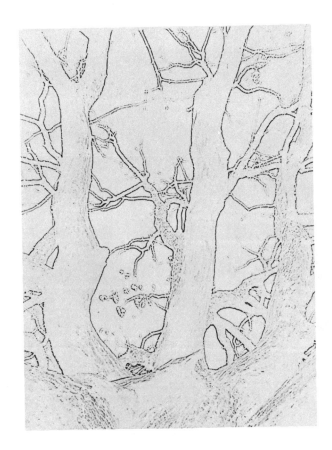

A word of explanation

The alternate structures in Part 1 are examples of some of the decisions that writers make. You are to change one standard structure to another standard structure according to each pattern provided. You are to imitate models. Starting with very simple patterns and ending with more complex ones, the exercises are designed to help you build a stockpile of structural choices for use in your own writing.

Part 1 has no systematic description of English grammar. You are not asked to supply such labels as "participle" or "noun phrase." There are no wrong structures, nor are any implied. You are not required to revise faulty writing. Instead, you will learn to write in much the same way as you learned to speak: you will imitate, repeat, and master various patterns of communication.

Patterns 1 through 12 present a range of alternate structures that function as parts of sentences, not as whole sentences. As you change one structure to another, you will come to understand various ways of expressing ideas within sentences. These patterns deal with possible decisions like the following:

IDEAS

The gestures are defiant.   Guards fear riots.

POSSIBLE DECISIONS OR ALTERNATE STRUCTURES

the defiant gestures   guards fearing riots
the gestures of defiance   riot-fearing guards
gestures that defy   guards who fear riots

THESE IDEAS WITHIN SENTENCES

Gestures that defy annoy riot-fearing guards.
The defiant gestures annoy guards who fear riots.

Patterns 1 through 62 in the second section of Part 1 stress entire sentences rather than structures within sentences.

As you convert one sentence pattern to another, notice the differences among alternate structures. Many of the alternates have essentially the same content, although punctuation and emphasis vary, as in the following examples:

1. The defiant gestures annoy the guards.
2. The guards are annoyed by the defiant gestures.
3. The gestures defy and annoy the guards.
4. The gestures are defiant; they annoy the guards.
5. The gestures being defiant, the guards are annoyed.

Other structures have words that introduce shades of difference in meaning as they relate ideas and sharpen emphasis:

1. *Because* the gestures are defiant, they annoy the guards.
2. The gestures are defiant; *therefore*, they annoy the guards.
3. Gestures, *when* defiant, annoy the guards.
4. The gestures are defiant, *however* annoying to the guards.
5. *The more* defiant the gestures, *the more* annoyed the guards.

Below is a suggested procedure for doing assignments in Part 1.

1. Study the models and the examples.
2. Read each item aloud; do each conversion orally.
3. Notice differences in word forms and in punctuation.
4. Write each conversion in the blank provided.
5. Be prepared for a class discussion comparing alternate structures. Ask yourself such questions as these:
   a. Are there any shades of difference in meaning?
   b. How does a shift in word order affect emphasis?
   c. What is the impact of repetition?
   d. What differences in tone do omissions make?
   e. How are balanced structures arranged?
   f. Why are balanced structures arranged this way?

Patterns within sentences

Pattern 1

MODEL   Love is an act of **endless forgiveness,** a tender look which becomes
a habit.   PETER USTINOV

A.	forgiveness without end	*endless forgiveness*
B.	theories about politics	*political theories*

1.   innocence without fear   _____

2.   problem in the suburbs   _____

3.   act of aggression   _____

4.   friends with influence   _____

5.   woman of discretion   _____

Pattern 2

MODEL   Williams' conversational stance is that of a six-foot-three-inch man under a **six-foot ceiling**.

JOHN UPDIKE

A.	ceiling that is six feet high	*six-foot ceiling*
B.	skeptics who have open minds	*open-minded skeptics*

1. jug that holds five gallons
2. blondes who have brown eyes
3. flat that has three rooms
4. animals that have short legs
5. lease that runs two years

Pattern 3

MODEL   We live in a mind-made world, where the things of prime importance are images or **words that embody ideas** and feelings and attitudes.

SUSANNE K. LANGER

A.	words embodying ideas	*words that embody ideas*
B.	mistake made by Tom	*mistake that Tom made*

1. computers matching couples
2. gang led by Fagin
3. drugs affecting vision
4. rocks collected by astronauts

Pattern 4

MODEL   Gazing up into the darkness, I saw myself as a **creature driven and derided by vanity**; and my eyes burned with anguish and anger.

JAMES JOYCE

A.   vanity-driven, vanity-derided creature

creature driven and derided by vanity

B.   hate-forged, hate-chiseled documents

documents forged and chiseled by hate

1.   fire-gutted, fire-decimated ghetto

2.   despair-molded, despair-hardened faces

3.   war-created, war-sustained prosperity

4.   custom-bound, custom-bridled tribes

Pattern 5

MODEL   Some had **blank, dumb, scrawny faces**, and their wives' faces matched. Some had twinkling eyes and could give out with **raucous, infectious laughter**.

CARL SANDBURG

A. blank faces that were dumb and scrawny

blank, dumb, scrawny faces

B. raucous laughter that was infectious

raucous, infectious laughter

1. harsh music that was irritating and endless

2. fragile beauty that was artificial

3. tough steak that was overcooked

4. short advertisements that were subtle and powerful

Pattern 6

MODEL   In the midafternoon the rain passed, and the sun was a disc of brass in a **cruelly bright sky**.   KATHERINE ANNE PORTER

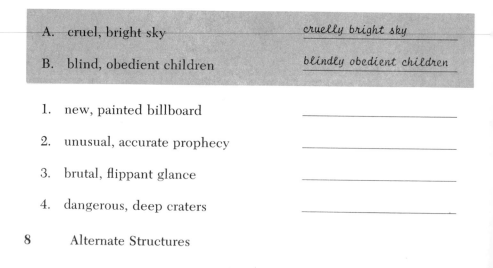

A. cruel, bright sky   *cruelly bright sky*

B. blind, obedient children   *blindly obedient children*

1. new, painted billboard

2. unusual, accurate prophecy

3. brutal, flippant glance

4. dangerous, deep craters

Pattern 7

MODEL   Francis stepped between them, gripping their armed fists, and they stared at him in a dull rage, **their eyes bloodshot and dangerously glittering.**   LOUIS DE WOHL

A. with their bloodshot, dangerously glittering eyes

their eyes bloodshot and dangerously glittering
_____

B. because of the murky, thoroughly polluted streams

the streams murky and thoroughly polluted
_____

1. with her straggly, carelessly applied eyelashes

_____

2. because of the inadequate, slowly vanishing food supply

_____

3. with their lithe, gracefully twisting bodies

_____

4. because of the unsavory, scarcely edible refreshments

_____

5. with their disruptive, deviously contrived strategy

_____

Pattern 8

MODEL   **One way to go quietly insane** is to think hard about the concept of eternity.   ERIC SEVAREID

A. one way that you can go quietly insane

   one way to go quietly insane
   _____

B. an editorial that should stifle opposition

   an editorial to stifle opposition
   _____

1. one way that you can get instant education
   _____

2. an argument that should end arguments
   _____

3. one question that you can ask Harvey
   _____

4. pills that should control the appetite
   _____

Pattern 9

MODEL   **What a man knows** is everywhere at war with **what a man wants.**

JOSEPH WOOD KRUTCH

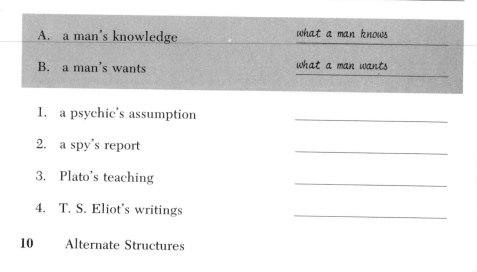

A. a man's knowledge   *what a man knows*
                                _____

B. a man's wants   *what a man wants*
                                _____

1. a psychic's assumption   _____

2. a spy's report   _____

3. Plato's teaching   _____

4. T. S. Eliot's writings   _____

Pattern 10

MODEL **Today's problems** are the products of **yesterday's successes.**
OSCAR HANDLIN

A. what are problems today   *today's problems*

B. what were successes yesterday *yesterday's successes*

1. what are swingers today   _____

2. what were flappers yesterday   _____

3. what was steak this morning   _____

4. what is hash tonight   _____

5. what were taboos last year   _____

Pattern 11

MODEL **To be idle** is no longer considered rewarding or even entirely respectable.
JOHN KENNETH GALBRAITH

A. their being idle   *to be idle*

B. your attending class *to attend class*

1. their being effusive _____

2. your clarifying an idea _____

3. their staying alert   _____

Patterns within Sentences   **11**

4. your admitting defeat _____

5. their standing firm _____

Pattern 12

MODEL **His saying something** made it true.   NORMAN COUSINS

A.	for him to say something	*his saying something*
B.	for them to drop out now	*their dropping out now*

1. for him to feign madness _____

2. for them to imitate us _____

3. for you to pamper her _____

4. for me to take the lead _____

5. for us to define *hippie* _____

SUMMARY OF PATTERNS

1. a. forgiveness without end ——— endless forgiveness
   b. theories about politics ——— political theories

2. a. ceiling that is six feet high ——— six-foot ceiling
   b. skeptics who have open minds ——— open-minded skeptics

3. a. words embodying ideas ——— words that embody ideas
   b. mistake made by Tom ——— mistake that Tom made

4. a. vanity-driven, vanity-derided creature ——— creature driven
      and derided by vanity
   b. hate-forged, hate-chiseled documents ——— documents
      forged and chiseled by hate

5. a. blank faces that were dumb and scrawny ——— blank, dumb, scrawny faces
   b. raucous laughter that was infectious ——— raucous, infectious laughter

6. a. cruel, bright sky ——— cruelly bright sky
   b. blind, obedient children ——— blindly obedient children

7. a. with their bloodshot, dangerously glittering eyes ——— their eyes bloodshot and dangerously glittering
   b. because of the murky, thoroughly polluted streams ——— the streams murky and thoroughly polluted

8. a. one way that you can go quietly insane ——— one way to go quietly insane
   b. an editorial that should stifle opposition ——— an editorial to stifle opposition

9. a. a man's knowledge ——— what a man knows
   b. a man's wants ——— what a man wants

10. a. what are problems today ——— today's problems
    b. what were successes yesterday ——— yesterday's successes

11. a. their being idle ——— to be idle
    b. your attending class ——— to attend class

12. a. for him to say something ——— his saying something
    b. for them to drop out now ——— their dropping out now

REVIEW EXERCISE 1

Review the Summary of Patterns to prepare for a class discussion of these questions:

1. Which conversions make a difference in meaning, not just in word order or emphasis?
2. Which conversions are structural changes only?
3. Give specific instances of shifts in word order that affect emphasis.

4. In Patterns 2 and 4, how does the hyphen aid the reader?
5. What does word order have to do with hyphenation?
6. How is number (singular *foot* and plural *feet*) related to word order and the hyphen?
7. In Pattern 6, what is the relationship of the comma to the *-ly* ending?
8. How is the comma related to *and* in Patterns 4, 5, and 7?
9. Why is the apostrophe used in Patterns 9 and 10?
10. In Pattern 12, what forms of *I, you, he, we,* and *they* appear before *to say* and *to drop out?* What forms appear before the *-ing* words in Patterns 11 and 12?

REVIEW EXERCISE 2

Make changes in structure according to the pattern of the examples.

A. Today **many children in America** plan to visit Mars.
      (grow up)

many American children
many children growing up in America
many children who grow up in America

Some leaders in Europe are considered diplomatic.
      (live in)

1. _____

2. _____

3. _____

B. Frank prefers **blondes with brown eyes.**
                          (have)

_____

brown-eyed blondes
blondes having brown eyes
blondes that have brown eyes

_____

Paul sketches **creatures with eight legs.**
                          (have)

4. _____

5. _____

6. _____

C. **Machines for stamping letters** are practical.

letter-stamping machines
machines to stamp letters

Campaigns for raising funds seem necessary.

7. _____

8. _____

D. Fads influenced **the decisions of the freshmen.**
(made)

the freshmen's decisions
what the freshmen decided
the decisions that the freshmen made
the decisions made by the freshmen

Who listened to **the suggestions of the women?**
(offered)

9. _____

10. _____

11. _____

12. _____

E. You have **practical ideas that are clear.**

clear, practical ideas
clearly practical ideas

They make **rigid regulations that are absurd.**

13. _____

14. _____

F. **His solutions** antagonized everyone.
    (present)

——

his presenting solutions
solutions presented by him
solutions that he presented

——

Their mistakes surprised no one.
    (make)

——

15. ————————————————————————————————

16. ————————————————————————————————

17. ————————————————————————————————

——

G. **The tardiness of all of us** was inexcusable.
        (be)

——

our being tardy
for us to be tardy
that we should be tardy

——

The eagerness of both of them seemed out of character.
        (be)

——

18. ————————————————————————————————

19. ————————————————————————————————

20. ————————————————————————————————

Patterns within Sentences   **17**

Patterns of sentences

Shifts in word order

While working with Patterns 1 through 7, notice the relationship of word order or arrangement to emphasis.

Pattern 1

A. Choice is emphasized by the very origin of the word *style*.

   The very origin of the word style emphasizes choice.

                                        CHARLES W. FERGUSON

B. The mood of helplessness was intensified by the darkness of day.

   The darkness of day intensified the mood of helplessness.

                                        ARTHUR M. SCHLESINGER, JR.

1. Even the bathroom was bugged by foreign agents.

   _____

2. Doubtful success and apparent failure were analyzed by Robert Browning.

   _____

   _____

3. Exotic snakes are kept as pets by some apartment dwellers.

　　_____

4. The number of abortions is influenced by the inflexible attitudes of parents.

　　_____

　　_____

5. The agony of the helpless is hidden by thick slaughterhouse walls.

　　_____

　　_____

Pattern 2

A. The idiotic certainties of ignorant men block free inquiry.

Free inquiry is blocked by the idiotic certainties of ignorant

men.

H. L. MENCKEN

B. A skillful thrust can penetrate the finest coat of mail.

The finest coat of mail can be penetrated by a skillful thrust.

HENRY MILLER

1. The theater of the absurd delights both young and old.

_____

2. Invisible hazards can cause fatal accidents.

_____

3. Empiricism, materialism, and rationalism strangle our
   intuitive powers.

_____

_____

4. Massive spraying can diminish the threat of encephalitis.

_____

_____

5. The hero of Robert Heinlein's *Stranger in a Strange Land*
   explains cannibalism.

_____

_____

Pattern 3

A. A primitive drum beat in the capital of technology land.

In the capital of technology land beat a primitive drum.

NORMAN MAILER

B. A half-promise of annihilation hangs over us.

Over us hangs a half-promise of annihilation.

PHYLLIS McGINLEY

1. Mysterious ruins stand on Salisbury Plain.

_____

2. Two pinpoints of light rolled across the midnight sky.

_____

3. A penalty marker lay near the two-yard line.

_____

4. The hope of immortality lingered in Tennyson's heart.

_____

5. The image of a black Christ flashed through my mind.

_____

Pattern 4

A. In Europe and Asia were burgeoning hideous political movements.

    Hideous political movements were burgeoning in Europe and

    Asia.

    JOHN FISCHER

B. Within us throbs the ache of unfulfilled experience.

    The ache of unfulfilled experience throbs within us.

    HERBERT GOLD

1. At the entrance of Dante's hell is a timely reminder.

    _____

2. To the nation's No. 3 team went the coveted Cotton Bowl bid.

    _____

3. Along the edge of the active volcano stood picture-taking tourists.

    _____

    _____

4. Behind those apparently complacent smiles are countless fears.

    _____

5. Out of one maze and into another run the frenzied status seekers.

    _____

    _____

Pattern 5

A. She reserved her overt superiority feelings for her friends.

Her overt superiority feelings she reserved for her friends.

MARY McCARTHY

B. I found the manifestations of Black Power depressing.

The manifestations of Black Power I found depressing.

ANTHONY BURGESS

1. He uses four-letter words only in the presence of his family.

2. She found the flowers of the desert fascinating.

3. They painted the hood of the green Maverick red and gold.

4. He repeats the punch line of one good joke all evening long.

When shifting the word order in sentences following Patterns 6 and 7, notice (a) the parallel structure of items in a series and (b) the arrangement of these items in order of climax or anticlimax.

Pattern 6

A. Tired feet, death, or debasement—here the alternatives were clear.

Here the alternatives were clear: debasement, death, or tired

feet.

JOHN OLIVER KILLENS

B. Setting race against race, employee against employer, nation against nation—the Communists have been following this tactic ever since.

The Communists have been following this tactic ever since:

setting nation against nation, employee against employer,

race against race.

HARRY AND BONARO OVERSTREET

1. A picnic, a formal banquet, or a rock festival—one of these activities will replace the usual carnival.

_____

_____

_____

2. Using glass for diamonds, brass for gold, chrome for silver —makers of costume jewelry have been perfecting this art for years.

_____

_____

_____

3. A Chihuahua, a black bear, or a Texas longhorn—one of these will be the mascot.

_____

_____

4. Equating a Volkswagen with a Mercedes Benz, Cuba with America, an imp with Mephistopheles—clever men use false analogies to persuade naive audiences.

_____

_____

_____

Pattern 7

A. I was all of these: acute and astute, perspicacious, calculating, keen.

Keen, calculating, perspicacious, acute and astute—

I was all of these.

MAX SHULMAN

B. Almost anything makes a deadly weapon in street combat: tire irons, lead pipes, steel chains, broken bottles.

Broken bottles, steel chains, lead pipes, tire irons—almost

anything makes a deadly weapon in street combat.

HARRISON E. SALISBURY

1. The feature articles were all of these: shrewd and lewd, ambiguous, scintillating, caustic.

_____

_____

2. Many things can dispel gloom on Monday morning: an effective tranquilizer, an atmospheric change, an unexpected letter, a heart-to-heart talk.

_____

_____

_____

3. They assumed the role of puppets: nameless and shameless, farcical, wooden, stupid.

_____

_____

4. Car advertisements feature similar appeals on television: easily swayed customers, suave salesmen, gorgeous girls.

_____

_____

_____

REVIEW

Keep in mind the following comments and questions as you review the Summary of Patterns.

1. Pattern 1 shifts a verb from the passive voice to the active, and Pattern 2 shifts a verb from the active voice to the passive. What is the difference in emphasis of ideas?
2. In a "loose sentence" main ideas appear first, but in a "periodic sentence" main ideas come last. Which sentences are periodic in Patterns 3 and 4? What does the position of ideas in a sentence have to do with emphasis?
3. In Pattern 5, which sentence has a natural word order? Which sentence departs from the usual word order? How does this departure affect emphasis of ideas?
4. In Patterns 6 and 7, could dashes replace the colons? What is the effect of the dash? Of the colon?

SUMMARY OF PATTERNS: Shifts in word order

1. FROM   Choice is emphasized by the very origin of the word *style*.
   TO   The very origin of the word *style* emphasizes choice.
   CHARLES W. FERGUSON
2. FROM   The idiotic certainties of ignorant men block free inquiry.
   TO   Free inquiry is blocked by the idiotic certainties of ignorant men.   H. L. MENCKEN
3. FROM   A primitive drum beat in the capital of technology land.
   TO   In the capital of technology land beat a primitive drum.
   NORMAN MAILER

4. FROM   In Europe and Asia were burgeoning hideous political movements.

   TO   Hideous political movements were burgeoning in Europe and Asia.   JOHN FISCHER

5. FROM   She reserved her overt superiority feelings for her friends.

   TO   Her overt superiority feelings she reserved for her friends.   MARY McCARTHY

6. FROM   Tired feet, death, or debasement—here the alternatives were clear.

   TO   Here the alternatives were clear: debasement, death, or tired feet.   JOHN OLIVER KILLENS

7. FROM   I was all of these: acute and astute, perspicacious, calculating, keen.

   TO   Keen, calculating, perspicacious, acute and astute— I was all of these.   MAX SHULMAN

REVIEW EXERCISE

Make changes in word order according to the pattern of the examples.

I. A. Our brains have been linked by chain thinking.

Chain thinking has linked our brains.

HARLOW SHAPLEY

B. The body of humanity has to thicken a man's individuality.

A man's individuality has to be thickened by the body

of humanity.

HARDIN CRAIG

1. The underpasses have been choked by flash floods.

_____

Shifts in Word Order   29

2. Lack of sleep has to affect a man's reflexes as well as his disposition.

3. The church rafters have been weakened by termites.

4. Reading great books should sharpen a person's diction as well as his wit.

II. A. The crummiest slums lie at the feet of the tallest and plushiest offices.

At the feet of the tallest and plushiest offices lie the crummiest slums.

E. B. WHITE

B. Still there under this new gaudy manner was the old personal charm.

The old personal charm was still there under this new gaudy manner.

JAMES JOYCE

5. The demolition crews came under the guise of progress and efficiency.

6. Always present even in his shortest greeting were
   the old innuendoes.

   _____

   _____

7. The best shops stand in the heart of the noisiest and
   dirtiest sections.

   _____

   _____

8. Still there under reams of old paper is his first
   diploma.

   _____

   _____

III. A. These might be called the "big four" of communica-
        tion: newspapers, radio, movies, and advertising.

        Newspapers, radio, movies, and advertising—these might

        be called the "big four" of communication.

                                        H. A. OVERSTREET

   B. Tenderness, joy, rage, anxiety—much of the inter-
      course between mother and child is the expression,
      on both sides, of feeling.

      Much of the intercourse between mother and child is the

      expression, on both sides, of feeling: tenderness,

      joy, rage, anxiety.

                                        LEWIS MUMFORD

9. These are among the giants of the musical world: Beethoven, Bach, Mozart, and Wagner.

    _____

    _____

10. Drilling, cleaning, welding, cutting—much of the mechanical work of ultrasonic waves was a marvel in the sixties.

    _____

    _____

Omissions and additions

When working with Patterns 8 through 20, notice how omitting or adding words affects emphasis. Also observe that (a) the omissions often tighten an expression and thus make for conciseness and (b) the additions may clarify ideas or may introduce significant differences in meaning.

Pattern 8

A. A kid today has everything. A kid today has everything except a private life.

   A kid today has everything—except a private life.

   AL CAPP

B. These men and women are up for election in November. They are up for election if they live until then.

   These men and women are up for election in November—if they

   live until then.

   STOKELEY CARMICHAEL

1. Single people today can save money. Single people today can save money for income taxes.

   _____

2. Chesterton says Christianity has not failed. He says Christianity has not failed because it has yet to be tried.

   _____

   _____

3. Any child can keep a secret. Any child can keep a secret in solitary confinement.

_____

_____

4. Scientists may create a better world. They may create a better world if they do not destroy it first.

_____

_____

5. Sykes will lend you anything. He will lend you anything for a price.

_____

_____

A. All books contain persuasion—communicate a selection of judgments about life.

All books contain persuasion. All books communicate a

selection of judgments about life.

GILBERT HIGHET

B. With this faith we will be able to hew out of the mountain of despair a stone of hope—to transform the jangling discords of our nation into a beautiful symphony of brotherhood.

With this faith we will be able to hew out of the mountain

of despair a stone of hope. With this faith we will be

able to transform the jangling discords of our nation into

a beautiful symphony of brotherhood.

MARTIN LUTHER KING, JR.

1. Our generation is not lost or beat—is not Machiavellian or Puritanical.

_____

_____

2. Do not fear change that buries falsehood alive—that digs up and revitalizes a true value.

_____

_____

_____

3. First-rate satirists delight in making us laugh at the petty games we play—in prodding us to change the rules.

_____

_____

_____

4. Galileo did not believe that rocks fall from the sky—that rocks could possibly be up there to fall.

_____

_____

_____

Pattern 10

A. The teacher is no longer a paid detective who is hunting stray commas.

The teacher is no longer a paid detective hunting stray commas.

JACQUES BARZUN

B. Pets that have been associated with human love and care have often shown a remarkable degree of psychic talent.

Pets associated with human love and care have often shown a

remarkable degree of psychic talent.

HANS HOLZER

1. Sports writers are no longer mere recorders that are xeroxing events on a playing field.

Sports writers are no longer mere _____

_____

2. Students that have been tuned in to current turbulence often make relevant suggestions.

_____ often

make relevant suggestions.

3. Louise likes to date the boys who are searching for a permanent cook.

Louise likes to date the _____

4. Legends of the deluge that have been told by American Indians parallel the story of Noah.

_____

_____ parallel the story of Noah.

Pattern 11

A. No one really involved in the landscape ever sees the landscape.

No one who is really involved in the landscape ever sees the

landscape.

B. Not every child possessing a phantasy world is possessed by it.

Not every child who possesses a phantasy world is possessed

by it.

BRUNO BETTELHEIM

1. The test given to unlicensed drivers is as hard as a final examination in cartography.

   _____ as hard
   as a final examination in cartography.

2. An unusual invitation offering free space to advertising agencies will bring immediate response.

   _____ to
   advertising agencies will bring immediate response.

3. The painting auctioned off for over a million dollars is a self-portrait.

   _____
   is a self-portrait.

4. A steam-powered car outperforming an ordinary gasoline-burning vehicle may soon help to clear the air.

   _____

   _____ may soon help to clear the air.

38   Alternate Structures

A. There is no aspect of human life that seethes with so many unexorcised demons as does sex.

No aspect of human life seethes with so many unexorcised

demons as does sex.

HARVEY COX

B. There were a million phrases of anger, pride, passion, hatred, tenderness that fought on his lips.

A million phrases of anger, pride, passion, hatred, tenderness

fought on his lips.

F. SCOTT FITZGERALD

1. There is not one of my friends who can identify with the characters of Hemingway or Faulkner.

_____ with the characters of Hemingway or Faulkner.

2. There were hundreds of litterbugs that were creating jobs for the county maintenance men.

_____ for the county maintenance men.

3. There is one sophomore who keeps analyzing Susy Smith's arguments for and against reincarnation.

_____ Susy Smith's arguments for and against reincarnation.

4. There were few Italians who remained unconcerned about the sinking of Venice and its treasures.

_____ about the sinking of Venice and its treasures.

Pattern 13

A. No dignity is like the dignity of a soul in agony.

There is no dignity like the dignity of a soul in agony.

EDITH HAMILTON

B. Blustering signatures swish across the page like cornstalks bowed before a tempest.

There are blustering signatures that swish across the pages

like cornstalks' bowed before a tempest.

F. L. LUCAS

1. No surprise is like the surprise of sudden death.

_____ of
sudden death.

2. Sizzling meats pop out hot grease like lidless percolators spewing out coffee.

_____ like
lidless percolators spewing out coffee.

3. No joy is like the joy of kissing and making up.

_____ of kissing and making
up.

4. Weary actresses leave the theater like tired racehorses limping off the track.

_____ like
tired racehorses limping off the track.

5. No pain is like the pain of lost love.

_____

Pattern 14

A.   It is the prestige symbols that must be changed.

The prestige symbols must be changed.

CLIFTON FADIMAN

B.   It is the beginning of wisdom to discover one's own biases.

To discover one's own biases is the beginning of wisdom.

S. I. HAYAKAWA

1.   It is fear that can paralyze the brain of a test-taker.

_____

2.   It is the job of a psychiatrist to interpret symbols in dreams.

_____

3.   It is the postal service that needs drastic improvement.

_____

4.   It was the aim of William Wilberforce to abolish slavery throughout the British Empire.

_____

_____

5.   It was Woodrow Wilson who was President of Princeton University in 1902.

_____

_____

Pattern 15

1. Benjamin West was a respected innovator, but he was not
    an imaginative painter.

    Benjamin West was a respected _____

    _____

2. T. H. Huxley was Darwin's bulldog; moreover, he was un-
    daunted by enemy attack.

    T. H. Huxley was Darwin's _____

    _____

3. A good dictionary is a record of current usage, but it is not
    a list of commandments.

    A good dictionary is a record of current _____

    _____

4. Too many idealists remain inactive dreamers; moreover,
    they stay disillusioned with an imperfect society.

    Too many idealists remain inactive _____

    _____

A. Old Mrs. Pomeroy memorialized the moment.

It was old Mrs. Pomeroy who memorialized the moment.

LIONEL TRILLING

B. To break the code of DNA in order to control human destiny is not necessary.

It is not necessary to break the code of DNA in order to

control human destiny.

LOREN EISELY

1. The Young Democrats congratulated the Young Republicans.

   _____

2. To give advice in order to promote one's vested interests is nothing new.

   _____

   _____

3. Robert Kennedy gave many Americans fresh hope.

   _____

4. To give the babies gifts in order to secure parental approval is not undiplomatic.

   _____

   _____

5. Wild flowers transform the roadside.

   _____

Pattern 17

A. We do discover them then—and only then—when they hurt someone or die.

Only when they hurt someone or die do we discover them.

JOHN STEINBECK

B. People will learn to reject the least in men at this time: when they know the best in men.

Only when people know the best in men will they learn to

reject the least in men.

MARYA MANNES

1. We do understand silent rejection then—and only then— when our friends freak out.

_____

2. They will live in a less hostile environment only at this time: when they opt for all-embracing love.

_____

_____

3. He does insist on playing another round then—and only then—when he has just won by a shutout.

_____

4. She will like being a housewife at that time: when she learns the value of routine chores.

_____

5. He will fully realize that a man's spirit never ages then— and only then—when he reaches sixty.

_____

Pattern 18

A. Even if the price of looking had been blindness, I would have looked.

Had the price of looking been blindness, I would have looked.
_____

RALPH ELLISON

B. If human problems were ever totally solved, change would come to a stop, and we would begin to die.

Were human problems ever totally solved, change would come to
_____

a stop, and we would begin to die.
_____

ERIC SEVAREID

1. Even if the result of leaving had been exile, Odysseus would have left.

_____

would have left.

2. If post offices were privately owned, rates would become competitive, and service would begin to improve.

_____ would

become competitive, and service would begin to improve.

3. Even if the effect of borrowing had been ruin, Abner would have borrowed.

_____

would have borrowed.

4. If weather patterns were under government control, democracy would be in danger, and no one would run for Congress.

_____

would be in danger, and no one would run for Congress.

Pattern 19

1. Because he was a rich and generous man, he provided well for his wife, and he poured thousands into trust funds for his children.

   _____

   _____ thousands into trust funds for his children.

2. Since she is astute, she naturally likes Nero Wolfe, and she is especially fond of Archie Goodwin.

   _____

   _____ fond of Archie Goodwin.

3. Because he is a patron of the arts, Mr. Jarvis always attends the symphony, and he never misses an opera.

   _____

   _____ an opera.

4. Since it is unsafe, the tool is no longer manufactured, and it will soon be removed from the market.

   _____

   _____ removed from the market.

Pattern 20

A. In football, players are bought by the pound. But in basketball, they are bought by the yard.

In football, players are bought by the pound; in basketball,

by the yard.

KENNETH EBLE

B. Suddenly his sickness seemed health. And his dizziness seemed to be stability.

Suddenly his sickness seemed health, his dizziness stability.

E. B. WHITE

1. To some, modern prophets are clever guessers. But to others, they are psychic phenomena.

   To some, modern prophets are clever _____

   _____

2. The boy's joy seemed arrogance. And his hard-won victory appeared to be sheer luck.

   The boy's joy seemed _____

   _____

   _____

3. In the beginning, his apology was a mistake in timing. But later, it was an error in judgment.

   In the beginning his apology was a mistake in _____

   _____

   _____ _____

4. Overeating may be indirect suicide. And heavy smoking may be a shortcut to purgatory.

Overeating may be indirect _____

_____

_____

REVIEW

As you review the Summary of Patterns, find examples of conversions that (1) introduce shades of difference in meaning, (2) affect the tone or mood, (3) repeat to emphasize an idea, (4) make for effective conciseness, (5) change punctuation to indicate an ellipsis.

SUMMARY OF PATTERNS: Omissions and additions

8. FROM A kid today has everything. A kid today has everything except a private life.

   TO A kid today has everything—except a private life.

   AL CAPP

9. FROM All books contain persuasion—communicate a selection of judgments about life.

   TO All books contain persuasion. All books communicate a selection of judgments about life.

   GILBERT HIGHET

10. FROM The teacher is no longer a paid detective who is hunting stray commas.

    TO The teacher is no longer a paid detective hunting stray commas. JACQUES BARZUN

11. FROM No one really involved in the landscape ever sees the landscape.

    TO No one who is really involved in the landscape ever sees the landscape. GEORGE ORWELL

12. FROM   There is no aspect of human life that seethes with so many unexorcised demons as does sex.

      TO   No aspect of human life seethes with so many unexorcised demons as does sex.   HARVEY COX

13. FROM   No dignity is like the dignity of a soul in agony.

      TO   There is no dignity like the dignity of a soul in agony.   EDITH HAMILTON

14. FROM   It is the prestige symbols that must be changed.

      TO   The prestige symbols must be changed.   CLIFTON FADIMAN

15. FROM   Thor Heyerdahl is a superb adventurer, but he is not a great writer.

      TO   Thor Heyerdahl is a superb adventurer, not a great writer.   JAMES A. MICHENER

16. FROM   Old Mrs. Pomeroy memorialized the moment.

      TO   It was old Mrs. Pomeroy who memorialized the moment.   LIONEL TRILLING

17. FROM   We do discover them then—and only then—when they hurt someone or die.

      TO   Only when they hurt someone or die do we discover them.   JOHN STEINBECK

18. FROM   Even if the price of looking had been blindness, I would have looked.

      TO   Had the price of looking been blindness, I would have looked.   RALPH ELLISON

19. FROM   Because he is a direct and active man, he is uncomfortable with introspection, and he seems embarrassed with a search for reasons.

      TO   A direct and active man, he is uncomfortable with introspection and seems embarrassed with a search for reasons.   LOUDON WAINWRIGHT

20. FROM   In football, players are bought by the pound. But in basketball, they are bought by the yard.

      TO   In football, players are bought by the pound; in basketball, by the yard.   KENNETH EBLE

REVIEW EXERCISE

Add or omit words according to the pattern of the examples.

A. Oscar Wilde doubted the validity of his own opinions. That is, he did
when everyone else agreed with him.

*Oscar Wilde doubted the validity of his own opinions—when
everyone else agreed with him.*
*It was Oscar Wilde who doubted the validity of his own opinions
when everyone else agreed with him.*
*Only when everyone else agreed with him did Oscar Wilde doubt
the validity of his own opinions.*

Portia questioned the legality of the bond. That is, she did when Shylock
remained unmoved.

1. _____

_____

2. _____

_____

3. _____

_____

B. In a library, silence can promote concentration. But at home, silence can promote misunderstanding.

In a library, silence can promote concentration; at home, misunderstanding.
Silence can promote concentration in a library. Silence can promote misunderstanding at home.

To the tourist, Hampton Court is an English palace. But to the historian, Hampton Court is the Henry-Wolsey arena.

4. _____

   _____

5. _____

   _____

C. Men overly worried about tomorrow waste their powers today.

Men who are overly worried about tomorrow waste their powers today.
There are men who worry overly about tomorrow and waste their powers today.
Were men overly worried about tomorrow, they would waste their powers today.

Students violently opposed to the machine-graded test advocate the classroom debate as a substitute.

6. _____

_____

7. _____

_____

8. _____

_____

D. There is no beauty like the beauty of clouds that vainly swirl to hide a sunset.

There is no beauty like the beauty of clouds vainly swirling to hide a sunset.
No beauty is like the beauty of clouds vainly swirling to hide a sunset.

There is no jealousy like the jealousy of a failure who constantly hopes to thwart another's success.

9. _____

_____

10. _____

_____

Questions and quotations

When asking questions or quoting the words of others, you may choose either the direct or the indirect forms. Notice in patterns 21 through 24 the shifts in word order, the omissions or additions, and the changes in punctuation.

Pattern 21

A. I wonder where freedom, justice, and integrity are now.

Where now are freedom, justice, and integrity?

GEORGE R. HARRISON

B. I ask what the moral difference is between putting an ear to a keyhole and bugging a room.

What is the moral difference between putting an ear to a keyhole and bugging a room?

RICHARD H. ROVERE

1. I wonder where the beatniks, the hippies, and the yippies are now.

_____

2. I ask what the basic distinction is between chanting "trick or treat" and saying "your money or your blood."

_____

3. I wonder where the aims, principles, and platform were then.

_____

4. I can guess what the real reasons were for his sudden retirement.

   _____

5. I wonder where the hand scythe, the two-seated bicycle, and the mail-order dreambook are now.

   _____

   _____

Pattern 22

A. But what would Leonardo da Vinci do in the century of the common man? (I wonder)

But I wonder what Leonardo da Vinci would do in the century of the common man.

HOWARD MUMFORD JONES

B. Why did the Copernican theory constitute a revolution in human thought? (This is)

This is why the Copernican theory constituted a revolution in human thought.

W. T. STACE

1. But what would Edison invent in the age of computers? (I wonder)

_____

2. Why did Thomas Paine go to Paris in 1792? (This is)

_____

3. And how does sunlight affect synthetic rubber? (I ask)

_____

4. Where is John Henry Newman buried? (That is)

_____

5. But why does the same author use both *op. cit.* and *ibid.*? (I wonder)

_____

Pattern 23

A. In a tone of moral superiority he said that he was ill.

"I am ill," he said in a tone of moral superiority.

GRAHAM GREENE

B. He said that there was a unicorn in the garden and added that the unicorn was eating roses.

"There's a unicorn in the garden," he said. "Eating roses."

JAMES THURBER

1. With tongue in cheek he said that he was a fink.

   _____

2. She said that there was a skeleton in the closet and added that the skeleton was reading *Frankenstein*.

   _____

   _____

3. In a spasm of self-pity she mumbled that she was all alone.

   _____

4. He said that there was a hired gunman in the house and added that the gunman was killing roaches.

   _____

   _____

5. With a frown of disapproval my father said that he did understand.

   _____

   _____

Pattern 24

A. "I celebrate myself," said Walt Whitman.

Walt Whitman said that he celebrated himself.

B. According to Norman Cousins, "Facts are terrible things if left sprawling and unattended." (thinks)

Norman Cousins thinks that facts "if left sprawling and

unattended" are terrible.

1. "I do not choose to run," announced Calvin Coolidge.

_____

2. According to the chef, "Mushrooms are irresistible if served steaming and unspiced." (says)

_____

_____

3. "I do not trust my own judgment," complained Mrs. Leary.

_____

4. According to our advisor, "Hatreds are contagious if left seething and unresolved." (believes)

_____

_____

5. "I say it with music," Fred added.

_____

REVIEW

Answer these questions as you review the Summary of Patterns.

1. At the end of a direct quotation, do commas and periods go inside or outside the quotation marks?
2. What word ordinarily precedes an indirect quotation?
3. How is word order related to direct and indirect questions?
4. What mark of punctuation ends an indirect question?

SUMMARY OF PATTERNS: Questions and quotations

21. FROM   I wonder where freedom, justice, and integrity are now.
    TO   Where now are freedom, justice, and integrity?
                                            GEORGE R. HARRISON

22. FROM   But what would Leonardo da Vinci do in the century of the common man? (I wonder)
    TO   But I wonder what Leonardo da Vinci would do in the century of the common man.
                                            HOWARD MUMFORD JONES

23. FROM   In a tone of moral superiority he said that he was ill.
    TO   "I am ill," he said in a tone of moral superiority.
                                            GRAHAM GREENE

24. FROM   "I celebrate myself," said Walt Whitman.
    TO   Walt Whitman said that he celebrated himself.

REVIEW EXERCISE

Change each direct question or quotation to an indirect one, and each indirect question or quotation to a direct one.

QUESTIONS

1. What is Lady Macbeth's tragic flaw? (I wonder)

2. I wondered how he lived to be one hundred and five.

_____

3. Why did Thomas More lose his head? (I ask)

_____

4. I asked how much hemlock Socrates drank.

_____

5. What is the secret of Santa Vittoria? (I wonder)

_____

QUOTATIONS

6. Sidney said, "I am glad that I was not born before tea."

_____

7. She insisted that she was not at all afraid.

_____

8. Job says, "I have spoken as fools speak."

_____

9. Edmund Wilson writes that he has had the same dream
over and over.

_____

10. Arnold's Empedocles cries out, "I will not judge!"

_____

Coordination and subordination

Patterns 25 through 40 show various ways to coordinate or subordinate ideas.

COORDINATION   Melodrama is honest; it does not mean to deceive.
EDGAR JOHNSON

(The structures before and after the semicolon have the same grammatical rank. Each can be written as a separate sentence: *Melodrama is honest. It does not mean to deceive.*)

SUBORDINATION   Since melodrama is honest, it does not mean to deceive.

(The structures before and after the comma do not have the same grammatical rank. The word *Since* before *melodrama is honest* makes the structure dependent on and grammatically subordinate to *it does not mean to deceive.*)

In the example above, subordination changes emphasis. In the following sentences, notice the differences in meaning as well as in emphasis.

All that matters about poetry is the enjoyment of it; however, it may be tragic.

All that matters about poetry is the enjoyment of it, however tragic it may be.
DYLAN THOMAS

Such connectives as *and, but, for, or, nor* and *however, in fact, moreover, nevertheless, otherwise, then,* and *therefore* are often used to link coordinate structures.

1. Let us never negotiate out of fear, *but* let us never fear to negotiate.
JOHN F. KENNEDY
2. Agriculture in these countries was not "advanced" technologically. *Nor* did it need to be.
PETER F. DRUCKER
3. To science the unknown is a problem full of interest and promise; *in fact* science derives its substance from the unknown. . . .
I. I. RABI

Connectives often mark the beginning of subordinate structures. The connectives most frequently used for this purpose are: *after, before, because, since, although, though, as, while, if, whether or not, as if, even if, when, where, unless,* and *until.* Subordinate structures may also begin with such words as *which, that,* or *who.*

1. *Whether or not* America is sick or violent, it surely is preachy; and one shares in this quality oneself, *as if* it were a public utility. WILFRED SHEED

2. The cheapest form of decoration is the unfamiliar word, *which* the speaker thinks must be elegant *because* it is unfamiliar to him. BERGEN EVANS

Important ideas may appear in subordinate structures as well as in coordinate ones.

Pattern 25

A. After they had stopped kissing and stood a little apart, mutual respect grew big in them.

They stopped kissing and stood a little apart. Mutual respect

grew big in them.

SHERWOOD ANDERSON

B. Because adults are children, they need to be loved in order to be good.

Adults are children. They need to be loved in order

to be good.

LOUIS EVELY

Coordination and Subordination **61**

1. After the leaders had met and talked peace for months, casualties doubled on the battlefront.

_____

_____

2. Since newspapers are educators, they should be accurate in order to be useful.

_____

_____

3. After Walter had sailed his seventh sea and won world acclaim, then his ship sprang a leak.

_____

_____

4. Because the Utah lake is a six-billion-ton reservoir, American salt cellars need not be empty for 2,000 years.

_____

_____

A. He opened the bathroom door. And he found himself face to face with an absolutely naked stranger. (When)

When he opened the bathroom door, he found himself face

to face with an absolutely naked stranger.

JOHN CHEEVER

B. Everything is emphatic. Therefore nothing is emphatic. (Where)

Where everything is emphatic, nothing is emphatic.

HAROLD WHITEHALL

1. She glanced out the window. And she saw a funnel cloud dip toward the courthouse. (When)

_____

_____

2. Nobody is the boss. So everybody is the boss. (Since)

_____

3. He raced down the alley. And he accidentally kicked a cat into the arms of an oncoming stranger. (As)

_____

_____

4. Mother is crabby. Therefore the whole family is crabby. (Because)

_____

5. The jet lifted off the runway. Then he remembered leaving his wallet on the ticket counter. (When)

_____

Coordination and Subordination   **63**

Pattern 27

A. Although people talk of the mysterious East, the West is also mysterious. (but)

People talk of the mysterious East, but the West is also

mysterious.

E. M. FORSTER

B. Since it must start with self-denial, the cure is harsh and likely to be unpopular. (for)

The cure is harsh and likely to be unpopular, for it must

start with self-denial.

JACQUES BARZUN

1. Although curiosity is an intellectual virtue, wild animals are often very curious. (but)

2. Since insects and disease have destroyed the lawn, Walter is now buying rocks and concrete. (for)

3. Even though Switzerland ranks highest with tourists, vacation lists show Great Britain and Italy not far from the top. (but)

4. Because he cannot measure or weigh God, he keeps his religion in a separate brain pocket. (for)

A. Mr. Lewis was a realist, but he occasionally saw life as through a glass darkly. (who)

Mr. Lewis was a realist who occasionally saw life as through a glass darkly.

EDWARD WEEKS

B. Some music reminds, and it does open the door to that imp of the concert hall, inattention. (that)

Music that reminds does open the door to that imp of the concert hall, inattention.

E. M. FORSTER

1. Mr. Ramsey is a bantam boxer, but he usually likes to throw his weight around. (who)

Mr. Ramsey is a bantam _____

_____

2. Some mothers smother, and they do make something out of their children, asthmatics. (that)

_____ something out of

their children, asthmatics.

3. Rudolph is an ardent socialist, but he does not want his own wealth distributed. (who)

Rudolph is an ardent _____

_____

_____

Coordination and Subordination **65**

4. The poison lasts, and it does contaminate the bodies of grass-eating animals, our meat. (that)

_____ the bodies

of grass-eating animals, our meat.

A. People in a hurry, since they can neither grow nor decay, are preserved in a state of perpetual puerility.

People in a hurry can neither grow nor decay; they are

preserved in a state of perpetual puerility.

ERIC HOFFER

B. Although scientific warfare was bad enough as it was, it is at least 10,000 times worse now.

Scientific warfare was bad enough as it was; it is at least

10,000 times worse now.

ANTHONY STANDEN

1. The winner in the mayor's race, since he claimed omniscience during the campaign, now has a problem.

_____

2. Although the council was bombarded by letters of protest, it still refused to act.

_____

3. Critics of the book, since they could neither understand nor interpret it, hesitated to recommend it.

_____

_____

4. Although Marvin refused to sell his painting, he gave it to the Salvation Army.

_____

_____

Coordination and Subordination　　67

Pattern 30

A. He stared at the camera; his eyes contradicted the flickering smile on his face. (*as* after *eyes*)

His eyes as he stared at the camera contradicted the

flickering smile on his face.

BERNARD MALAMUD

B. He had one mistress, music; he was faithful to her to the day of his death. (*whom* for *her*)

He had one mistress to whom he was faithful to the day of his

death: music.

DEEMS TAYLOR

1. He devoured the stock market report; his indigestion was painfully evident. (*as* after *indigestion*)

   His _____

   _____

2. He hated one man, himself; he could never be kind to himself. (*whom* for *himself*)

   He hated one _____

   _____

3. She was boarding the jet; her friends teased her about lurking hijackers. (*as* after *friends*)

   Her _____

   _____

4. He gave her one gift, a wedding band; the price tag was dangling from it. (*which* for *it*)

   He gave her one _____

   _____

Pattern 31

A. We become as we follow the paths of science constantly more aware of mysteries beyond scientific reach.

Following the paths of science, we become constantly more aware

of mysteries beyond scientific reach.

CHARLES A. LINDBERGH

B. The mountains' vast sterility that had been changed by the alchemy of a dream was transformed into magnificence.

Changed by the alchemy of a dream, the mountains' vast

sterility was transformed into magnificence.

JOHN KEATS

1. Students discover as they acquire more and more knowledge how much there is yet to learn.

_____

_____ how much there is yet to learn.

2. The balloons that had been sent up by weathermen looked like flying saucers.

_____

3. He demonstrates when he trains young technicians the need for service apart from salary.

_____

the need for service apart from salary.

4. The boy who was challenged by the gigantic task was ready to clean the stables.

_____

to clean the stables.

Pattern 32

A. Sweeping from one spot to another, cruelty's like a searchlight.

Cruelty's like a searchlight. It sweeps from one spot to

another.

GRAHAM GREENE

B. Having shot an unarmed man, he found life more terrible and difficult than death.

He found life more terrible and difficult than death. He had

shot an unarmed man.

JOSEPH CONRAD

1. Mechanically adhering to one track, his mind is like a monorail.

   His _____

2. Having forgotten the speaker's name, the chairman talked on and on and on.

   The chairman _____

   _____

3. Flashing on and off, ESP is like a warning indicator.

   ESP _____

4. Having spoken the language all his life, Philip saw no reason to take any English course.

   Philip _____

   _____

A. A good teacher feels his way and looks for response.

A good teacher feels his way, looking for response.

PAUL GOODMAN

B. A foolish consistency is the hobgoblin of little minds and is adored by little statesmen and philosophers and divines.

A foolish consistency is the hobgoblin of little minds, adored

by little statesmen and philosophers and divines.

RALPH WALDO EMERSON

1. A fair contract prevents strikes and keeps men on the job.

A fair contract _____

2. The pass was intercepted and became the most important play of the Super Bowl.

The pass was intercepted _____

_____

3. The officer uses his competent thumb and unravels the traffic knot.

The officer uses his _____

4. Trusilla is the fraternity sweetheart and is envied by her roommate, her lab partner, and her best friend.

Trusilla is the fraternity _____

_____

Pattern 34

1. Australia is not the hangout of hotheads. But it is not the abode of the blessed either.

   Australia is _____

   _____

2. The father when present was not strict. And he did not see any need for discipline.

   The father _____

   _____

3. The marriage bond was not made of steel. But it was not made of angel's hair either.

   The marriage bond _____

   _____

4. That misanthrope does not like any man. And he does not show any concern for other animals.

   That misanthrope _____

A. The bus stopped with a sudden jerk, shaking him from his meditation.

The bus stopped with a sudden jerk and shook him from his

meditation.

FLANNERY O'CONNOR

B. Mrs. Miller stiffened, opening her eyes to a dull, direct stare.

Mrs. Miller stiffened and opened her eyes to a dull, direct

stare.

TRUMAN CAPOTE

1. The empty bottle fell to the pavement, sending jagged glass in all directions.

The empty bottle fell to _____

_____ in all directions.

2. Mr. Shaver talks in his sleep, moaning weirdly in the dark silence.

Mr. Shaver talks _____

_____ in the dark silence.

3. Frank intercepted the long pass, creating the break that led to victory.

Frank intercepted _____

_____ that led to victory.

4. We ambled down the midway, gnawing our corn on the cob.

We ambled down _____

Pattern 36

A. We have not really conquered nature. Nor have we conquered ourselves. (because)

We have not really conquered nature because we have not

conquered ourselves.

LOREN EISELEY

B. A space traveler cannot avoid the Milky Way. Nor could I have bypassed Texas easily. (about as . . . as)

I could have bypassed Texas about as easily as a space

traveler can avoid the Milky Way.

JOHN STEINBECK

1. Johnny has not learned to write. Nor has he learned to read. (because)

Johnny _____

_____

2. A Beatle fan cannot give up rock music. Nor could Edward have happily foregone rich desserts. (about as . . . as)

Edward _____

_____

3. He will not win an Olympic race. Nor does he intend to train for it. (since)

He will _____

4. An egalitarian cannot fraternize with an aristocrat. Nor could my parents have endorsed middle-class mediocrity willingly. (almost as . . . as)

My parents _____

_____ with an aristocrat.

A. The ghetto subjected to a state of siege, citizens can no longer move freely into and out of their neighborhoods.

The ghetto is subjected to a state of siege. Citizens can

no longer move freely into and out of their neighborhoods.

RALPH W. CONANT

B. Memory being notoriously unreliable, witnesses are not to be trusted.

Memory is notoriously unreliable. Witnesses are not to be

trusted.

MARTIN EBON

1. Her hair sprinkled with confetti, she is looking for the powder room.

_____

_____

2. The bus being reasonably dependable, we usually get to class on time.

_____

_____

3. The golf course invaded by moles, officials postponed the finals.

_____

4. The telephone jangling constantly, Mr. Hurley cannot concentrate.

_____

Coordination and Subordination   **75**

Pattern 38

A. His eyebrows were raised high in resignation. He began to examine his hands.

His eyebrows raised high in resignation, he began to examine

his hands.

LIONEL TRILLING

B. I bled from both nose and mouth. The blood spattered upon my chest.

I bled from both nose and mouth, the blood spattering upon

my chest.

RALPH ELLISON

1. His integrity was questioned by the heirs. He decided to resign as guardian.

   His _____

   _____ to resign as guardian.

2. Melton campaigned from hovel to penthouse. His energy shamed our lethargy.

   Melton _____

   _____ our lethargy.

3. His pleas were denied by the court. He resorted to tantrums.

   His pleas _____ tantrums.

4. Mr. Boltzer mixed three languages. His manuscripts challenged translators.

   Mr. Boltzer _____

   _____ translators.

Pattern 39

A. His orchestration is elaborate. The melody of his thought is lost.
    (so . . . that)

    His orchestration is so elaborate that the melody of his

    thought is lost.

    JOHN MASON BROWN

B. Ahab is a hero. *Moby Dick* itself is a heroic book. (Just as . . . so)

    Just as Ahab is a hero, so Moby Dick itself is a heroic book.

    ALFRED KAZIN

1. The mail was sluggish. I received one Christmas card on January
    25. (so . . . that)

    The mail _____

    _____

2. His protagonist flees every danger. The author himself is
    an escapist. (Just as . . . so)

    _____

    _____

3. The child is truthful. He needs muffling at times. (so . . . that)

    _____

4. The moon moves. The tides ebb and flow. (As . . . so)

    _____

5. Mr. Davis is tall. His bald head hardly shows. (so . . . that)

    _____

Pattern 40

1. He seems to think more of his own importance when he yells louder. _____

2. As the clock becomes more important, it is more likely to spawn mechanical men. _____

3. One appears to be more angelic when one is younger.

_____

4. If his allowance is more generous, then he will be more likely to share it with others. _____

5. When our copper is more plentiful, then it is more apt to drop in price. _____

Study the following Summary of Patterns. Be prepared to answer in class such questions as these: Is the semicolon used between structures of equal or unequal grammatical rank? Are semicolons and periods interchangeable? What mark of punctuation often follows an introductory subordinate element? When is a comma used between coordinated ideas?

Also be prepared to write original sentences modeled on any patterns that your instructor may select.

UMMARY OF PATTERNS: Coordination and subordination

25.	FROM	After they had stopped kissing and stood a little apart, mutual respect grew big in them.
	TO	They stopped kissing and stood a little apart. Mutual respect grew big in them. SHERWOOD ANDERSON
26.	FROM	He opened the bathroom door. And he found himself face to face with an absolutely naked stranger. (When)
	TO	When he opened the bathroom door, he found himself face to face with an absolutely naked stranger. JOHN CHEEVER
27.	FROM	Although people talk of the mysterious East, the West is also mysterious. (but)
	TO	People talk of the mysterious East, but the West is also mysterious. E. M. FORSTER
28.	FROM	Mr. Lewis was a realist, but he occasionally saw life as through a glass darkly. (who)
	TO	✳ Mr. Lewis was a realist who occasionally saw life as through a glass darkly. EDWARD WEEKS
29.	FROM	People in a hurry, since they can neither grow nor decay, are preserved in a state of perpetual puerility.
	TO	People in a hurry can neither grow nor decay; they are preserved in a state of perpetual puerility. ERIC HOFFER
30.	FROM	He stared at the camera; his eyes contradicted the flickering smile on his face. (*as* after *eyes*)
	TO	His eyes as he stared at the camera contradicted the flickering smile on his face. BERNARD MALAMUD
31.	FROM	We become as we follow the paths of science constantly more aware of mysteries beyond scientific reach.
	TO	Following the paths of science, we become constantly more aware of mysteries beyond scientific reach. CHARLES A. LINDBERGH

32. FROM   Sweeping from one spot to another, cruelty's like a searchlight.

     TO   Cruelty's like a searchlight. It sweeps from one spot to another.   GRAHAM GREENE

33. FROM   A good teacher feels his way and looks for response.

     TO   A good teacher feels his way, looking for response.
     PAUL GOODMAN

34. FROM   England is not the jeweled isle of Shakespeare's much-quoted passage. But it is not the inferno depicted by Dr. Goebbels either.

     TO   England is not the jeweled isle of Shakespeare's much-quoted passage, nor is it the inferno depicted by Dr. Goebbels.   GEORGE ORWELL

35. FROM   The bus stopped with a sudden jerk, shaking him from his meditation.

     TO   The bus stopped with a sudden jerk and shook him from his meditation.   FLANNERY O'CONNOR

36. FROM   We have not really conquered nature. Nor have we conquered ourselves. (because)

     TO   We have not really conquered nature because we have not conquered ourselves.   LOREN EISELEY

37. FROM   The ghetto subjected to a state of siege, citizens can no longer move freely into and out of their neighborhoods.

     TO   The ghetto is subjected to a state of siege. Citizens can no longer move freely into and out of their neighborhoods.   RALPH W. CONANT

38. FROM   His eyebrows were raised high in resignation. He began to examine his hands.

     TO   His eyebrows raised high in resignation, he began to examine his hands.   LIONEL TRILLING

39. FROM   His orchestration is elaborate. The melody of his thought is lost. (so . . . that)

     TO   His orchestration is so elaborate that the melody of his thought is lost.   JOHN MASON BROWN

40. FROM   One learns to believe more in the very real existence of evil as one gets older.

     TO   The older one gets, the more one learns to believe in the very real existence of evil.
     LAWRENCE FERLINGHETTI

REVIEW EXERCISE

Fill in blanks according to the patterns of the examples.

A.   Rod ploughed through his notes. He underscored sections in red.

Ploughing through his notes, Rod underscored sections in red.
Rod as he ploughed through his notes underscored sections in red.
Rod ploughed through his notes and underscored sections in red.
As Rod ploughed through his notes, he underscored sections in red.
Rod ploughed through his notes; he underscored sections in red.

Dan stalked across the stage. He tripped over a bucket.

1.   _____ —

_____

2.   _____ —

_____

3.   _____ —

_____

4.   _____ —

_____

5.   _____ —

_____

B. His last name is not Duffy. But it is not Durfey either.

His last name is not Duffy, nor is it Durfey.
His last name is not Duffy; it is not Durfey either.
If his last name is not Duffy, it is not Durfey either.

Her first novel was not a best seller. But it was not a failure either.

6. _____

_____

7. _____

_____

8. _____

_____

C. After the fire had been smothered, the fishermen moved on downstream.

The fire smothered, the fishermen moved on downstream.
The fishermen who had smothered the fire moved on downstream.
The fishermen smothered the fire and then moved on downstream.
The fishermen moved on downstream. They had smothered the fire.
Having smothered the fire, the fishermen moved on downstream.

After his ego had been punctured, the girl offered him a band-aid.

9. _____

_____

10. _____

_____

11. _____

_____

12. _____

_____

13. _____

_____

D. Silas hit the brakes hard and spun the car around fast.

Silas hit the brakes hard, spinning the car around fast.
When Silas hit the brakes hard, he spun the car around fast.
Silas hit the brakes so hard that he spun the car around fast.
The harder Silas hit the brakes, the faster the car spun around.

She keeps the budget low and runs her savings high.

14. _____

_____

15. _____

_____

16. _____

_____

17. _____

_____

E. Alex cannot see without glasses. And his father could not see clearly with bifocals.

Alex cannot see without glasses; moreover, his father could not see clearly with bifocals.
Alex cannot see without glasses, nor could his father see clearly with bifocals.
His father could see with bifocals about as clearly as Alex can see without glasses.

Nancy cannot read poetry. And her husband could not easily read prose.

18. _____ —

_____

19. _____ —

_____

20. _____ —

_____

Parallelism and arrangement

Structures that are parallel look alike. A single word or a word group may have essentially the same structure as another part of the sentence. Sentences themselves may be parallel.

SINGLE WORDS

a. Neither *intelligence* nor *integrity* can be imposed by law.
    CARL L. BECKER
b. Millions of consumers are *manipulated, razzle-dazzled, indoctrinated, mood-conditioned,* and *flimflammed.*   VANCE PACKARD

WORD GROUPS

a. New Salem stood on a hill, *a wrinkle of earth crust, a convulsive knob of rock and sod.*   CARL SANDBURG
b. The problem in a democracy is not *to assimilate minorities* but *to avoid stifling them* as they attain their equality.
    NORMAN MAILER
c. The validity of an idea has nothing to do with *who propounds it*—or *whom it outrages.*   LEO ROSTEN
d. *Journalism allows its readers to witness history; fiction gives its readers an opportunity to live it.*   JOHN HERSEY

SENTENCES

a. Women think you are trying to make a pick-up. Men fear you intend to lift their wallets.   RICHARD L. NEUBERGER
b. Our minds can detect remote similarities and build up large patterns of thought. Their minds cannot make those jumps and fill in those connections.   GILBERT HIGHET

Parallel items in a series—whether single words, word groups, or sentences—often have a discernible, logical order or arrangement.

1. Three fundamental questions of an intelligent human being are: Where did I come from? Who am I? Where am I going? (Time order)   ADRIAN V. CLARK

2. The university is not an employment agency; it is not an adjunct of corporations; it is not an instrument of government. (From small to large) HENRY STEELE COMMAGER

3. One swaps tranquillizers, like recipes. One samples them, like mints. One grades them, like vintage wines. (Time order and climax) LOUIS KRONENBERGER

As you convert one structure to another in this section, give special attention not only to the various kinds of parallelism but also to the arrangement of ideas.

Pattern 41

The ghetto ferments. It is paradoxical. In it are conflicts and dilemmas.

The ghetto is ferment, paradox, conflict, and dilemma.

KENNETH B. CLARK

1. The tumult rages. It is treacherous. Within it are miseries and mutinies.

———————————————————————————

———————————————————————————

2. First love dazzles. It is delirious. With it come illusions and muddles.

———————————————————————————

———————————————————————————

Parallelism and Arrangement 87

Pattern 42

A man runs after a hat. He is not half so ridiculous as one who runs after a wife.

A man running after a hat is not half so ridiculous as a man running after a wife.

G. K. CHESTERTON

1. A woman minces an apple. She is not nearly so distracting as one who minces words.

   _____

   _____

2. A freshman brags about his grades. He is not half so noisy as one who brags about his girls.

   _____

   _____

Pattern 43

From every side came the roaring of the flames. Walls crashed. Dynamite was detonated.

From every side came the roaring of the flames, the crashing

of walls, and the detonations of dynamite.

JACK LONDON

1. In his memory churned the flashing of the headlights. Brakes screeched. The driver was confused.

_____

_____

2. From every speaker blared the yelling of the crowds. Bands played. The score was repeated.

_____

_____

Pattern 44

When we really love a person, we never judge him. (means)

To love a person means never to judge him.

LOUIS EVELY

1. Whenever they rigidly enforce the letter of the law, they kill the spirit of the law. (is)

_____

Parallelism and Arrangement   89

2. If we give money, we give of ourselves. (means)

_____

_____

Pattern 45

At first he seemed vital and clever, shrewd and political; we thought he was a populist. We have come to see him as a man who is violent and devious, who is both cynical and hypocritical, who is a paranoiac. (not . . . but)

We have come to see him as not vital but violent, not clever

but devious, not shrewd but cynical, not political but

hypocritical, not populist but paranoiac.

JULES FEIFFER

1. At first they seemed cold and aloof, selfish and remote; she felt they were her enemies. She came to regard them as people who were warm and helpful, who were both generous and affable, who were dependable friends.

She came to regard them _____

_____

_____

2. Our dream home was to be spacious and sprawling, bright and airy; we imagined it a two-story mansion. We have come to live in a place that is crowded and small, that is both dark and musty, that is a two-room basement apartment.

We have come to live in a place _____

_____

_____

Pattern 46

The evidence is already in. We have compromised ourselves fatally. The role of the individual is either to destroy society or drop out of it. The alienated feel that all this is true.

The alienated feel that the evidence is already in, that we

have compromised ourselves fatally, and that the role of the

individual is either to destroy society or drop out of it.

RICHARD ROVERE

1. The battle is not worth fighting. Defeat is inevitable. The proper course of action is either to whine or sulk. The pessimist feels this way.

   The pessimist _____

   _____

   _____

2. Public utilities should reach every house in the country. Natural gas should be piped in. There should be pure water for everyone. My father believes all this.

   My father _____

   _____

   _____

Pattern 47

A haggard face suddenly appeared at the window of our car. The eyes were bloodshot, and the skin was pasty white under a three days' beard.

A haggard face—eyes bloodshot, skin pasty white under a three

days' beard—suddenly appeared at the window of our car.

MALCOLM COWLEY

1. Unexpected guests piled into our kitchen. Their suitcases were bulging, and their stomachs were empty after a long, cold drive.

   _____

   _____

   _____

2. A tiny girl stood at the door. Her smile was forced, and her hands were filled with gingham potholders from her mother's machine.

   _____

   _____

   _____

Pattern 48

For the Japanese were by no means alone in feeling that progress in weapons meant two things. Not only did it mean better killing, but it also diminished human stature.

For the Japanese were by no means alone in feeling that

progress in weapons (a) meant better killing and (b)

diminished human stature.

NOEL PERRIN

1. But the conservationists are not the only men believing that preservation of forests involves two things. Not only does it involve constant reseeding, but it also requires more national forests.

   But the conservationists are not the only men believing that

   _____

   _____

2. And George Bernard Shaw said that marriage offers two things. Not only does it offer much temptation, but it also provides many opportunities to yield.

   And George Bernard Shaw said that _____

   _____

   _____

Pattern 49

Just as the symbol is NOT the thing symbolized, the word is NOT the thing any more than the map is the territory it stands for.

The symbol is NOT the thing symbolized; the word is NOT the thing; the map is NOT the territory it stands for.

S. I. HAYAKAWA

1. Just as the intention is NOT the deed, the blueprint is NOT a home any more than the pattern is a new dress.

———————————————————————

———————————————————————

———————————————————————

2. Just as a warning is NOT a catastrophe, a news bulletin is NOT a hurricane any more than the two-minute whistle is the end of a football game.

———————————————————————

———————————————————————

———————————————————————

Pattern 50

As the Kerner Report warned, we're heading toward two Americas. One of these is white, rich, and educated. The other is black, poor, and uneducated.

As the Kerner Report warned, we're heading toward two

Americas: one white, one black; one rich, one poor; one

educated, one uneducated.

JOHN O'CONNOR

1. While the assembly listened, leaders debated two plans of action. One of these was practical, timely, constructive. The other was nebulous, archaic, and imprudent.

_____

_____

_____

2. As the yearbook had predicted, the twins were seeking different goals. One sought a farm, a tractor, and a frugal wife. The other sought an office, a computer, and a competent secretary.

_____

_____

_____

Parallelism and Arrangement   95

Pattern 51

Law cannot help the deliberate homicide because he defies it. The would-be suicide rejects medicine, which cannot help him. The hardened atheist disbelieves religion; therefore, religion cannot help him.

Law cannot help the deliberate homicide. He defies it.

Medicine cannot help the would-be suicide. He rejects it.

Religion cannot help the hardened atheist. He disbelieves it.

MAX RAFFERTY

1. Advice cannot move the stubborn man because he ignores it. The ranter scorns silence, which displeases him. The proud spirit mocks humility; therefore, humility cannot touch him.

2. Billboard warnings will not slow us down because we do not read them. We do not buckle our safety belts, which will not save us. We do not obey the laws; therefore, they will not diminish fatalities.

REVIEW

As you study the following Summary of Patterns, underline parallel structures. Be prepared to write original sentences modeled on any patterns that your instructor may select.

SUMMARY OF PATTERNS: Parallelism and arrangement

41. FROM   The ghetto ferments. It is paradoxical. In it are conflicts and dilemmas.

     TO   The ghetto is ferment, paradox, conflict, and dilemma.
                                         KENNETH B. CLARK

42. FROM   A man runs after a hat. He is not half so ridiculous as one who runs after a wife.

     TO   A man running after a hat is not half so ridiculous as a man running after a wife.   G. K. CHESTERTON

43. FROM   From every side came the roaring of the flames. Walls crashed. Dynamite was detonated. (of)

     TO   From every side came the roaring of the flames, the crashing of walls, and the detonations of dynamite.
                                         JACK LONDON

44. FROM   When we really love a person, we never judge him. (means)

     TO   To love a person means never to judge him.
                                         LOUIS EVELY

45. FROM   At first he seemed vital and clever, shrewd and political; we thought he was a populist. We have come to see him as a man who is violent and devious, who is both cynical and hypocritical, who is a paranoiac. (not . . . but)

     TO   We have come to see him as not vital but violent, not clever but devious, not shrewd but cynical, not political but hypocritical, not populist but paranoiac.
                                         JULES FEIFFER

46. FROM   The evidence is already in. We have compromised ourselves fatally. The role of the individual is either to destroy society or drop out of it. The alienated feel that all this is true.

TO   The alienated feel that the evidence is already in, that
        we have compromised ourselves fatally, and that the
        role of the individual is either to destroy society or
        drop out of it.   RICHARD ROVERE

47. FROM   A haggard face suddenly appeared at the window of
            our car. The eyes were bloodshot, and the skin was
            pasty white under a three days' beard.

    TO   A haggard face—eyes bloodshot, skin pasty white
            under a three days' beard—suddenly appeared at the
            window of our car.   MALCOLM COWLEY

48. FROM   For the Japanese were by no means alone in feeling
            that progress in weapons meant two things. Not only
            did it mean better killing, but it also diminished hu-
            man stature.

    TO   For the Japanese were by no means alone in feeling
            that progress in weapons (a) meant better killing and
            (b) diminished human stature.   NOEL PERRIN

49. FROM   Just as the symbol is NOT the thing symbolized, the
            word is NOT the thing any more than the map is the
            territory it stands for.

    TO   The symbol is NOT the thing symbolized; the word
            is NOT the thing; the map is NOT the territory it
            stands for.   S. I. HAYAKAWA

50. FROM   As the Kerner Report warned, we're heading toward
            two Americas. One of these is white, rich, and edu-
            cated. The other is black, poor, and uneducated.

    TO   As the Kerner Report warned, we're heading toward
            two Americas: one white, one black; one rich, one
            poor; one educated, one uneducated.

                                                 JOHN O'CONNOR

51. FROM   Law cannot help the deliberate homicide because he
            defies it. The would-be suicide rejects medicine,
            which cannot help him. The hardened atheist dis-
            believes religion; therefore, religion cannot help him.

    TO   Law cannot help the deliberate homicide. He defies
            it. Medicine cannot help the would-be suicide. He
            rejects it. Religion cannot help the hardened atheist.
            He disbelieves it.   MAX RAFFERTY

REVIEW EXERCISE 1

Use various types of parallel structures according to the pattern of the examples.

A. If one writes out an argument, he thinks it through.

To write out an argument is to think it through.
Write out an argument; think it through.
One who writes out an argument is one who thinks it through.

If one studies for a test, he builds self-confidence.

1. _____

2. _____

3. _____

_____

B. We can learn history when we read books. We can also learn history when we see movies and watch TV.

We can learn history by reading books, seeing movies, and watching TV.
By reading a book, seeing a movie, or watching a TV program, we can learn history.
Read books. See movies. Watch TV. Learn history.

They can win games when they practice plays and develop precision.
They can win when they obey the training rules.

4. _____

_____

5. _____

_____

6. _____

_____

C. Education should draw out. It should not just pour into.

Education should draw out rather than pour into.
Education that draws out is better than education that pours into.
To draw out, not pour into—that is what education should do.
Education is at its best when drawing out, not when pouring into.

A writer should look into. He should not just look at.

7. _____

8. _____

9. _____

10. _____

REVIEW EXERCISE 2

Fill in blanks with items that parallel the structures printed in bold face.

a. **To lose one game** is not _to lose the conference._

b. Elmo sat **beside Mary** and _behind Frank._

c. My lawyer knew **what to say,** _what to do._

1. Thomas enjoys **taking walks** and _____

2. The lost keys may be **in a drawer** or _____

3. **To serve others** is _____

4. Neither **the green skirt** nor _____

   looked good with those shoes.

5. Not only **does George fret about unpaid bills,** but _____

   also _____

6. He said **that he had read the ode,** _____

   _____

7. I wanted to know **who he was** and _____

8. Peace will come **when we negotiate with the enemy,** ____

   _____

9. **The torchlight parade started at 6:30 p.m.;** _____

   _____

10. **Can an eagle swim?** Or _____

   _____

Connection and division

When rewriting or revising, an author may decide to replace several short sentences with one longer one to connect and relate ideas more closely. Or he may choose to break one long sentence into several short ones to divide ideas for emphasis. The use of connection or division relates not only to emphasis but also to tone or mood.

Pattern 52

Since his honor is saved, he remains a great man, and once again the industry triumphs; in fact, not only is the dignity of life preserved, but everything is hotsytotsy.

His honor is saved. He remains a great man. Once again the

industry triumphs. The dignity of life is preserved.

Everything is hotsytotsy.

WILLIAM SAROYAN

1. When the doorbell rang at midnight, I remembered the news report, and I was afraid; however, not only did I open the door, but the escaped convict walked in.

2. After I had failed my botany test, I lost my history notes, and once again I faced a *D*; moreover, the bus was late, and my supper was cold: the next day was Friday the thirteenth.

> Cholera appears in Egypt. Planes come in. They sail in from every nation. They come to banish the curse.
>
> *When cholera appears in Egypt, planes from every nation come sailing in to banish the curse.*
>
> SEAN O'CASEY

1. The moon-walkers visited our town. We came crowding in. We wanted to touch these miracle men. _____

   _____

   _____

2. The Review Committee assembled in the lounge. Nell came in. She marched in to hear the debate.

   _____

   _____

   _____

Various combinations

Instead of converting one structure to another in this section, you are asked to write sentences having essentially the same structure as each model given. Supply your own words and ideas as you demonstrate not only your mastery of the patterns set forth in preceding sections but also your ability to combine these patterns.

a. The only advice we seem to get from Salinger is to be charming on the way to the loony bin. PHILIP ROTH

The only vacation he seems to approve of at the moment is to

go threading through the Rockies on horseback.

b. No matter how much responsible student self-government emerges, it still remains true that a modern university cannot be a republic of equals. LEWIS S. FEUER

No matter how many times democracy has failed, it still is a

fact that no other political system has more respect for the

freedom and the dignity of the individual.

c. Human beings are peculiar; when they are not sure that what they are saying is true, they say it louder and with greater conviction. LUCY EISENBERG

Some women shoppers are unpredictable; when they are sure that

they like a certain dress, they still want to try on

everything else on the rack.

Pattern 54

All mortals tend to turn into the thing they are pretending to be.
C. S. LEWIS

Pattern 55

There is more tragedy than humor in this illusion that a turban makes
a man different.   HARRY GOLDEN

_____

_____

_____

Pattern 56

An octopus inhabits the nebula, an octopus whose twisting, waving
arms are bundles of magnetic lines of force.

                          JOHN ARCHIBALD WHEELER

_____

_____

_____

Pattern 57

A statue may be nude, but it is almost never naked; conversely we do
not use *nude* as a substitute in the phrase *the naked truth*.

                          CHARLTON LAIRD

_____

_____

_____

Pattern 58

Plants that act like animals and animals that resemble plants, matter that is living and at the same time not living—all are inhabitants of the strange environment of the soil.　　　　　PETER FARB

_____

_____

_____

_____

Pattern 59

Although many had American weapons, a large number of the short, frail-looking men had homemade guns wrought from pipes fastened to hand-whittled wooden stocks.　　　　　WILLIAM LEDERER

_____

_____

_____

_____

Pattern 60

Within the New Left, clear lines are drawn between the "old New Left" (approximate age, thirty), the New Left (between twenty-two and twenty-eight) and the "new New Left" or "young kids" (under twenty-two).   KENNETH KENISTON

Pattern 61

No one can censor the erotic, for no one can repeal psychology; no one can censor the suggestive, for no one can predict individual response; and no one can censor the salacious, for the tone of the voice and the expression of the face and body are beyond legislation.

BERNARD DE VOTO

Pattern 62

The flower in the crannied wall when pulled out of its cranny—and what child would dream of not pulling it out?—inevitably turns into God and man.　　　　　　　　　　　GEORGE BOAS

_____

_____

_____

_____

Ways to Develop Paragraphs

A word of explanation

In expository and argumentative writing, and often in descriptions and narratives, many paragraphs have a similar structure. At or near the beginning comes a sentence that contains a key idea. Next is a group of unified sentences that develop this key idea. (Some writers end this type of paragraph with a sentence that clinches or drives home the main point; others omit the clincher.) You may decide to use this structure for many of your own paragraphs.

But it is by no means the only choice you have. If you prefer an inductive approach, you can begin a paragraph with specifics and then add other specifics that lead up to a final generalization. Or, if you wish, you can omit the generalization; you can unify your ideas in such a way that your main point is clearly implied rather than stated.

When planning and writing a paragraph, you may choose to use only one method of developing a key idea or to combine two or more methods. For instance, you may present specific facts, or you may combine facts with examples. You may write one paragraph that defines, another that summarizes, and still another that analyzes. Or you may write one paragraph that combines definition, summary, and analysis.

Part 2 presents twenty model paragraphs that illustrate methods often used to develop ideas. Following each paragraph are several activities. The *analyses* may be individual written assignments or springboards for class discussions. The *structures for study* (selected sentences from model paragraphs) not only review sections of Part 1 but also introduce new combinations of patterns and stylistic variations. These structures may be used as dictation exercises. The sections on *diction* are intended to direct attention to the significance of word choice. Finally, the *assignments* are suggestions only. Although they specify written work, they may be converted to oral exercises; paragraphs containing examples, specific details, classifications, and definitions are especially suitable for oral development in class.

Emphasis here is always on method—on *how* an idea may be developed. The more methods you know, the wider your range of choices will be.

Paragraph 1

Americans, very many of them, are obsessed with tensions. Nerves are drawn tense and twanging. Emotions boil up and spill over into violence largely in meaningless or unnatural directions. In the cities people scream with rage at one another, taking out their unease on the first observable target. The huge reservoir of the anger of frustration is full to bursting. The cab driver, the bus or truck driver, pressed with traffic and confusion, denounces Negroes and Puerto Ricans unless he is a Negro or a Puerto Rican. Negroes burn up with a hateful flame. A line has formed for the couches of the psychoanalysts of people wound so tight that the mainspring has snapped and they deliver their poisons in symbolic capsules to the doctor. The legal and criminal distribution of sleeping pills and pep pills is astronomical, the first opening escape into sleep and the second access to a false personality, a biochemical costume in which to strut. Kicks increasingly take the place of satisfaction. Of love, only the word, bent and bastardized, remains.   JOHN STEINBECK

ANALYSIS

1. The first sentence of the paragraph is a topic sentence. Underline in it the key words that Steinbeck develops.
2. What emotions relate to tensions?
3. What actions indicate obsession?
4. What specific examples show that "the anger of frustration is full to bursting"?
5. How do *capsules, pills, satisfaction,* and *love* relate to the key idea in the first sentence?

STRUCTURE FOR STUDY

"The legal and criminal distribution of sleeping pills and pep pills is astronomical, the first opening escape into sleep and the second access to a false personality, a biochemical costume in which to strut."

From AMERICA AND AMERICANS by John Steinbeck, Copyright © 1966 by John Steinbeck. All rights reserved. Reprinted by permission of The Viking Press, Inc.

DICTION

Give the meaning in context of (1) *drawn tense and twanging*, (2) *a biochemical costume*, and (3) *love . . . bent and bastardized.*

ASSIGNMENT

Write a paragraph based on your observations of one characteristic of Americans. Or write a paragraph beginning with one of the following sentences; develop the italicized ideas.

1. College *students*, a significant number of them, *are* restless gadflies *pestering the Administration.*
2. Having already found identity, *many a freshman is happily "doing his own thing."*
3. *Clothes* no longer make the man, but they do *indicate a man's philosophy.*

Paragraph 2

Dehumanization is a patent fact of life. Loneliness increases as the machine, symbolized by the computer, takes over America and, week by week, decreases human contacts: automatic elevators, drive-in banking without visible human tellers, TV check-ins at motels, recorded voices on the phone or issuing commands and advice from ceilings and walls, TV lectures to huge classes at universities. Some of the devices have a sinister aspect. Samples: At Boston's Logan Airport, a camera with winking lights sweeps across a baggage area. An adjacent sign warns: "This area is under Constant Electronic Surveillance for the protection of your property." At a nearby rental-car counter, another camera and another sign: "For your protection, a confidential film is being made of this transaction." In frantic search for personal involvement amid this inanimate insulation of society, people are plunging into such deeply emotional experiments as encounter sessions, sensitivity training, T-groups and "immersion" weekends.   FLETCHER KNEBEL

ANALYSIS

1. Where does the controlling idea of the paragraph first appear?
2. What machines does Knebel choose to discuss? List a few of the machines that he decided *not* to mention.
3. What specific examples does he give of dehumanizing machines in action? Do these examples have parallel structure? Which structures before colons are elliptical (words omitted that are necessary for the complete grammatical construction but are not required for understanding the sentence)? In these what words does a reader easily supply?
4. Find and underline a very short sentence that is not only emphatic but also transitional.
5. Relate the last sentence to the first sentence.

STRUCTURE FOR STUDY

"In a frantic search for personal involvement amid this inanimate insulation of society, people are plunging into such deeply emotional experiments as encounter sessions, sensitivity training, T-groups and 'immersion' weekends."

DICTION

Give the meaning in context of (1) *dehumanization*, (2) *a sinister aspect*, and (3) *this inanimate insulation*.

ASSIGNMENT

Fill in this blank with a word of your own (a word like *Change* or *Joy*): "_____ is an important part of everyday living." Begin a paragraph with the sentence, and develop it with specific examples. You may prefer to begin with and develop one of the following sentences:

1. Sensitivity training can (*or* cannot) humanize us.
2. Old prejudices are wearing new masks.
3. Not every four-letter word is obscene.

The fight crowd is a beast that lurks in the darkness behind the fringe of white light shed over the first six rows by the incandescents atop the ring, and is not to be trusted with pop bottles or other hardware. The tennis crowd is the pansy of all the great sports mobs and is always preening and shushing itself. The golf crowd is the most unwieldy and most sympathetic, and is the only horde given to mass production of that absurd noise written generally as "tsk tsk tsk tsk," and made between tongue and teeth with head-waggings to denote extreme commiseration. The baseball crowd is the most hysterical, the football crowd the best-natured and the polo crowd the most aristocratic. Racing crowds are the most restless, wrestling crowds the most tolerant, and soccer crowds the most easily incitable to riot and disorder. Every sports crowd takes on the characteristics of the individuals who compose it. Each has its particular note of hysteria, its own little cruelties, mannerisms, and bad mannerisms, its own code of sportsmanship and its own method of expressing its emotions.   PAUL GALLICO

ANALYSIS

1. Instead of stating the controlling idea first and developing it with specific details, how does Paul Gallico begin and end his paragraph?
2. Notice that parallelism links and unifies ideas; underline the parallel beginnings of sentences.
3. Show the organization of Paragraph 3 by listing in order the specific details: (a) the fight crowd, a not-to-be-trusted beast ... (b) the tennis crowd, a preening and shushing pansy ... and so on.

STRUCTURE FOR STUDY

"The golf crowd is the most unwieldy and most sympathetic, and is the only horde given to mass production of that absurd noise written generally as 'tsk tsk tsk tsk,' and made between tongue and teeth with head-waggings to denote extreme commiseration."

From A LARGE NUMBER OF PERSONS by Paul Gallico. *Vanity Fair*, September, 1931. Copyright © 1931 by Condé Nast Publications. Reprinted by permission of Harold Ober Associates, Incorporated.

DICTION

Instead of using "a beast that *stays* in the darkness," Gallico chose "a beast that *lurks* in the darkness." What other words might he have selected for (1) *incandescents*, (2) *preening and shushing*, (3) *extreme commiseration*, and (4) *easily incitable to riot?*

ASSIGNMENT

Write a paragraph that lists four or five specifics first and ends with a generalization that links these specifics. Here are a few suggested endings:

1. Every salesman has his own mannerisms, his own special tricks.
2. College classes have distinct personalities.
3. All bad drivers seem to be afflicted with varying degrees of insanity.

Paragraph 4

The October hurricane proved the old adage about the want of the nail for which the shoe was lost. The littlest violation of the building codes, the most minor skimping of material—nails too far apart or too small, mortar too poor or too sparingly used, a roofing felt lighter than the prescribed kind, flashing of too thin a gauge let in a finger of the tempest, and the hand and brawny arm thrust in behind. A tile rattled and flipped into the night; the tiles above it were plowed loose. Metal began to vibrate and then tore; the material beneath ballooned, ripped, raced into oblivion, and the roof after it, and then, sometimes, the walls buckled. In days to come, Miami would learn new lore concerning building against hurricanes and learn, shamefacedly, that among its capable builders there were a few cheats. Some people lost everything because a contractor had saved himself as little as ten dollars on a home.   PHILIP WYLIE

From HOW TO LIVE THROUGH A HURRICANE by Philip Wylie. *The Saturday Evening Post,* December 30, 1950. Reprinted with permission of *The Saturday Evening Post.* Copyright © 1950, Curtis Publishing Co.

ANALYSIS

1. Where does the key idea first appear? Is there a clincher sentence?
2. How does Philip Wylie organize the evidence that supports his main point? What section of the paragraph has time order?
3. Underscore parallel structures that follow the dash.

STRUCTURE FOR STUDY

"Metal began to vibrate and then tore; the material beneath ballooned, ripped, raced into oblivion, and the roof after it, and then, sometimes, the walls buckled."

DICTION

Point out effective word choice, especially words indicating action—such as *rattled, flipped, plowed loose.*

ASSIGNMENT

Using Paragraph 4 as a model, present organized modern evidence to support the validity of an old adage. Below are suggested adages from Benjamin Franklin's *Poor Richard's Almanac:*

1. There are no gains without pains.
2. Now I have a sheep and a cow, everybody bids me good morrow.
3. If you would have a faithful servant, and one that you like, serve yourself.

Paragraph 5

Much modern poetry is difficult. Some of it may be difficult because the poet is snobbish and definitely wants to restrict his audience, though this is a strange vanity and much rarer than Mr.

Eastman would have us think. Some modern poetry is difficult because it is bad—the total experience remains chaotic and incoherent because the poet could not master his material and give it a form. Some modern poetry is difficult because of the special problems of our civilization. But a great deal of modern poetry is difficult for the reader simply because so few people, relatively speaking, are accustomed to reading *poetry as poetry*. The theory of communication throws the burden of proof upon the poet, overwhelmingly and at once. The reader says to the poet: Here I am; it's your job to "get it across" to me—when he ought to be assuming the burden of proof himself.   CLEANTH BROOKS

ANALYSIS

1. What four reasons does Cleanth Brooks list to support his topic sentence?
2. When do explanatory details accompany reasons? Why?
3. Underscore repeated words that contribute to the unity of the paragraph.

STRUCTURE FOR STUDY

"Some modern poetry is difficult because it is bad—the total experience remains chaotic and incoherent because the poet could not master his material and give it form."

DICTION

Give the meaning in context of (1) *strange vanity*, (2) *the total experience remains chaotic and incoherent*, and (3) *reading poetry as poetry*.

ASSIGNMENT

Write a paragraph in which you state the main idea in the first sentence. Then develop the controlling idea with three or four supporting reasons. Here are some suggested topic sentences:

1. Bridging a generation gap is difficult.
2. We must explore outer space.
3. Television will never be a good substitute for books.

Poverty in America does not mean starvation. It does not mean utter destitution, hunger, or homelessness as it does for hundreds of millions of the poor of Asia, Africa, and Latin America. But it does mean substandard medical care, substandard education, and substandard cultural influences, all of which doom the children of the poor to remain poor unless blessed by extraordinary ability or great good fortune. It means a shorter life plagued by more frequent physical and mental disease; a smaller body and a less developed mind. And it means passing aimless days on street corners and the porches of rural shacks. It means stagnation.   EDWARD BROOKE

ANALYSIS

1. Compare Edward Brooke's definition of poverty in America with this definition of *poverty* in the *Standard College Dictionary:* "1. The condition or quality of being poor or without sufficient subsistence. 2. Scantiness of supply: a *poverty* of imagination. 3. Absence or scarcity of necessary qualities, elements, etc.: *poverty* of soil."
2. Why is the last sentence of Paragraph 6 especially emphatic? Compare the last sentence with the first.
3. In the fourth sentence, what words does the reader easily supply just after the semicolon?
4. Point out specific instances of these transitional devices in Paragraph 6: parallel structures, repeated words, connectives at the beginning of sentences.

STRUCTURE FOR STUDY

"But it does mean substandard medical care, substandard education, and substandard cultural influences, all of which doom the children of the poor to remain poor unless blessed by extraordinary ability or great good fortune."

DICTION

1. What does Brooke write instead of *poverty means doing nothing for days?*
2. What specific details does the final word *stagnation* emphasize or clinch?

From WHERE I STAND by Edward Brooke. *The Atlantic Monthly*, March, 1966. Reprinted by permission of the author.

ASSIGNMENT

Write a paragraph that defines. First state what something is not; then tell what it is. Place the strongest part of your definition last. Here are some suggested topics:

1. wealth in America
2. poverty of spirit
3. black power
4. grades on transcripts

Paragraph 7

It all turned out kind of like the way the architect in Evelyn Waugh's *Decline and Fall* describes life as being like one of those whirling discs at the old amusement parks. You get on the disc and it starts spinning and the faster it goes, the more centrifugal force builds up to throw you off it. The speed on the outer edge of the disc is so fast, you have to hold on for dear life just to stay on but you get a hell of a ride. The closer you can get to the center of the disc, the slower the speed is and the easier it is to stand up. In fact, theoretically, at the very center there is a point that is completely motionless. In life, some people won't get on the disc at all. They just sit in the stands and watch. Some people like to get on the outer edge and hang on and ride like hell—that would be Gossage and Feigen. Others are standing up and falling down, staggering, lurching toward the center. And a few, a very few, reach the middle, that perfect motionless point, and stand up in the dead center of the roaring whirligig as if nothing could be clearer and less confused—That would be McLuhan. TOM WOLFE

ANALYSIS

1. According to Tom Wolfe, what do life and a whirling disc have in common?
2. Relate various places on or off the disc to various commitments of people in life.

From THE NEW LIFE OUT THERE by Thomas K. Wolfe, Jr. Reprinted by permission of Thomas K. Wolfe, Jr. c/o Marvin Josephson Associates, Inc. Copyright © 1965 The New York *Herald Tribune*, Inc.

3. In the third sentence, a comma is substituted for what word?
4. Why do you suppose Wolfe chose *that* after the first dash and *That* after the second dash?

STRUCTURE FOR STUDY

"The closer you can get to the center of the disc, the slower the speed is and the easier it is to stand up."

DICTION

Give the meaning of these words in context: (1) *centrifugal*, (2) *theoretically*, (3) *lurching*, and (4) *whirligig*.

ASSIGNMENT

Using Paragraph 7 as a model, write a paragraph presenting a detailed comparison. Some suggested beginnings for the comparisons are:

1. Life is like a rock festival.
2. That trip on the train was like a ride in a submarine.
3. Matthew Arnold was right when he said that modern life—with "its sick hurry" and "its divided aims"—is a strange disease.
4. Their behavior reminds me of a drag race.

Paragraph 8

Progress by dissent then is characteristic of human societies. It has been responsible for the growth and success of democracy in the last four hundred years, and the decline and failure of absolute forms of government. For the crucial feature of democracy is not simply that the majority rules, but that *the minority is free to persuade people* to come over to its side and make a new majority. Of course, the minority is abused at first—Socrates was, and so was

From PROTEST—PAST AND PRESENT by Jacob Bronowski. *The American Scholar,* Volume 38, Number 4, Autumn, 1969. Copyright © 1969 by the United Chapters of Phi Beta Kappa. Reprinted by permission of the publishers.

Charles Darwin. But the strength of democracy is that the dissident minority is not silenced; on the contrary, it is the business of the minority to convert the majority; and this is how a democratic society invigorates and renews itself in change as no totalitarian society can.

JACOB BRONOWSKI

ANALYSIS

1. Relate every sentence in Paragraph 8 to "progress by dissent."
2. Find instances of Jacob Bronowski's use of transitional devices: (a) such words as *it* and *this* referring to preceding words or ideas, (b) such connectives as *and, for,* and *but,* as well as such transitional expressions as *of course* and *on the contrary,* (c) repetition of key words like *democracy* and of key ideas like "absolute forms of government."

DICTION

1. What are *"absolute* forms of government"?
2. Are the words *invigorates* and *renews* synonyms?
3. What is a *"crucial* feature," a *"dissident* minority"?

STRUCTURE FOR STUDY

"For the crucial feature of democracy is not simply that the majority rules, but that *the minority is free to persuade people* to come over to its side and make a new majority."

ASSIGNMENT

Use various transitional devices to link your ideas as you develop a paragraph with explanatory details. You might begin with one of the following sentences:

1. Minorities use nonviolence effectively to persuade the majority.
2. Assassination of a leader makes no sense in the United States.
3. There are reasons for the silence of the majority.
4. Education by osmosis is the best education.

For years I have had a recurrent dream. I take a road that runs toward the west. It is summer; I pass by a strange summer forest, in which there are mysterious beings, though I know that, on the whole, they are shy and benign. If I am fortunate and find the way, I arrive at a wonderful river, which runs among boulders, with rapids, between alders and high weedy trees, through a countryside fresh, green and wide. We go in swimming; it is miles away from anywhere. We plunge in the smooth flowing pools. We make our way to the middle of the stream and climb up on the pale round gray stones and sit naked in the sun and the air, while the river glides away below us. And I know that it is the place for which I have always longed, the place of wildness and freedom, to find which is the height of what one may hope for—the place of unalloyed delight.   EDMUND WILSON

ANALYSIS

1. Observe the effect of the *I* approach or point of view.
2. What is the effect of the quick shift to the *we* approach?
3. What logical arrangement of details does Edmund Wilson use?

STRUCTURE FOR STUDY

"We make our way to the middle of the stream and climb up on the pale round gray stones and sit naked in the sun and the air, while the river glides away below us."

DICTION

1. What words does the author choose to make his readers see and feel?
2. What abstract words appear in the last sentence?

ASSIGNMENT

Write a paragraph describing one of your own interesting dreams. If you do not remember any, then write about an actual but misty memory. Pay special attention to word choice. Arrange details in order of time. If appropriate, end the paragraph with the impression the dream leaves on your waking senses.

From THE OLD STONE HOUSE in *The American Earthquake* by Edmund Wilson. Copyright © 1958 by Edmund Wilson, Doubleday & Co., Inc.

Paragraph 10

Our festering dumps and air-poisoning incinerators are "a national disgrace," says the Public Health Service; and in the garbage explosion itself, a Chicago expert sees looming cataclysm: "We're running in front of an avalanche, and it's already begun to bury us." In the rhetoric of waste-disposal men, this notion of literal burial recurs with dismaying regularity. "People are up to their knees in garbage, but they don't really care," says a New York specialist. "In three more years, when they're up to their waists in it, they'll start screaming."

FRANK TRIPPETT

ANALYSIS

1. When presenting three quotations, what logical order does Frank Trippett use?
2. What is the function of the sentence without a direct quotation? What words make a transition from one quotation to the next?
3. What controlling idea is clearly implied?

STRUCTURE FOR STUDY

"'People are up to their knees in garbage, but they don't really care,' says a New York specialist. 'In three more years, when they're up to their waists in it, they'll start screaming.'"

DICTION

1. In the first sentence, what word might have been used instead of *festering?* what instead of *air-poisoning?*
2. Relate the meaning and the order of *garbage explosion, looming cataclysm,* and *avalanche.*
3. What does "the *rhetoric* of waste-disposal men" mean?

From THE EPIC OF GARBAGE by Frank Trippett. By courtesy of the editors. From the November 4, 1969 issue of *Look Magazine.* Copyright © 1969 by Cowles Communications, Inc.

ASSIGNMENT

Write a paragraph presenting three or four closely related quotations or facts. Instead of stating your controlling idea, imply it. The following is a list of suggested ideas:

1. Sonic booms anger earth-bound citizens.
2. Taxes are now a great burden.
3. Protestants, Catholics, and Jews have one important belief in common.
4. One-car accidents are often suicide attempts.

Paragraph 11

Now the love of flowers is a very misleading thing. Most women love flowers as possessions, and as trimmings. They can't look at a flower, and wonder a moment, and pass on. If they see a flower that arrests their attention, they must at once pick it, pluck it. Possession! A possession! Something added on to *me!* And most of the so-called love of flowers today is merely this reaching out of possession and egoism: something I've *got:* something that embellishes *me.* Yet I've seen many a collier stand in his back garden looking down at a flower with that odd, remote sort of contemplation which shows a *real* awareness of the presence of beauty. It would not even be admiration, or joy, or delight, or any of those things which so often have a root in the possessive instinct. It would be a sort of contemplation: which shows the incipient artist.   D. H. LAWRENCE

ANALYSIS

1. Briefly summarize the different reactions to flowers.
2. How does D. H. Lawrence show rather than merely talk about the women's reactions?
3. How does he analyze each reaction?

From NOTTINGHAM AND THE MINING COUNTRYSIDE by D. H. Lawrence. In *Phoenix: The Posthumous Papers of D. H. Lawrence*, edited by Edward D. McDonald. Reprinted by permission of The Viking Press, Inc.

STRUCTURE FOR STUDY

"And most of the so-called love of flowers today is merely this reaching out of possession and egoism: something I've *got:* something that embellishes *me.*"

DICTION

1. Is *egoism* a good synonym for *egotism?*
2. Is *meditation* an exact synonym for *contemplation?*
3. What is the difference between "the *potential* artist" and "the *incipient* artist"?

ASSIGNMENT

Using Paragraph 11 as a model, state two different reactions to something; explain and analyze each reaction. Here are a few suggested beginnings:

1. A poet and an astronomer see a sunset through different eyes.
2. To some, money is a means; to others, an end.
3. An atheist and a Christian react differently as they look at a crucifix.

Paragraph 12

Typical of Einstein is the story of the popular lecture he was finally prevailed upon to give, for it shows his incapability of behavior that was not genuine. He had been asked many times to speak to a certain audience, but had always begged off on the basis that he had nothing to say. Finally, however, the pressure became so great that he was forced to accede. Came the evening of the lecture, and amidst applause Dr. Einstein was led to the front of the stage and introduced. For a few moments he looked out at the audience, tongue-tied and silent. Finally he could stand it no longer and, smiling sheepishly, said, "I find that I have nothing to say," and returned to his seat.   GEORGE R. HARRISON

From ALBERT EINSTEIN: APPRAISAL OF AN INTELLECT by George R. Harrison. *Atlantic Monthly*, June, 1955. Reprinted by permission of the author.

ANALYSIS

1. Why does George R. Harrison choose this incident to tell rather than another?
2. What do you think that he means by "not genuine"?
3. Had Einstein been capable of "behavior that was not genuine," how would you change the ending of the incident?

STRUCTURE FOR STUDY

"For a few moments he looked out at the audience, tongue-tied and silent."

DICTION

1. Define in context *prevailed upon* and *forced to accede*.
2. Why do you suppose Harrison chose *he had been asked, he was forced to accede,* and *Dr. Einstein was led to the front* instead of *friends had asked him, they forced him to accede,* and *the chairman led Dr. Einstein?*

ASSIGNMENT

Write a paragraph developing an idea with an incident. Begin by giving your reason for deciding upon that particular incident. Supply interesting details. You may wish to begin with one of these ideas:

1. Typical of my friend is a story of the way he borrowed a hundred dollars from a miser by means of his ability to talk his way through almost any predicament.
2. The following incident shows how his oversolicitousness frustrates his roommate.
3. My mother enjoys comedy based on a situation rather than on linguistic prowess; one of her favorite stories deals with . . . .

Paragraph 13

The human being says that the beast in him has been aroused, when what he actually means is that the human being in him has been aroused. A person is not pigeon-toed, either, but person-toed, and what the lady has are not crow's-feet but woman-wrinkles. It is our species, and not any other, that goes out on wildcat strikes, plays the badger game, weeps crocodile tears, sets up kangaroo courts. It is the man, and not the shark, that becomes the loan shark; the cat burglar, when caught, turns out not to be a cat but a man; the cock-and-bull story was not invented by the cock and the bull; and the male of our species, at the height of his arrogant certainties, is mansure and not cocksure, just as, at his most put-upon, he is woman-nagged and not hen-pecked.   JAMES THURBER

ANALYSIS

1. What idea underlies Thurber's stated main point?
2. What false notion does he mention in order to contradict?
3. Would his contradiction be as convincing if only four or five of the best illustrations were used? In an abridgment, which would you delete?
4. Can you think of other examples that Thurber may have deliberately omitted?

STRUCTURE FOR STUDY

"It is our species, and not any other, that goes out on wildcat strikes, plays the badger game, weeps crocodile tears, sets up kangaroo courts."

DICTION

1. What synonyms are used for *human being?*
2. Why do you suppose that *crow's-feet* is combined with *woman-wrinkles* instead of with *woman's wrinkles?*

ASSIGNMENT

Using Paragraph 13 as a guide, write a paragraph presenting evidence to refute an idea stated at the beginning. Like Thurber, you will have two ideas (one positive and the other negative) to discuss, and you may find parallel structures especially useful. Supply copious, specific, carefully selected examples that emphasize your point of view.

You might choose to begin with one of the following ideas:

1. Many straightforward individuals believe that they always use straightforward language, but they do not. In letters to absolute strangers, for example, they start with "Dear Sir" when they mean "Hey, you, whether you are a man or a woman."
2. The self-righteous are convinced that their self-labels are accurate, when in reality these labels are sheer inversions. Such persons refer to their dignity rather than to their obvious lack of humility.
3. Some men consider the Woman's Liberation Movement much ado about nothing, but I know better.

Paragraph 14

It is an extraordinary thing to watch the sand come to life if one happens to be wading where there is a large colony of the crabs. One moment it may seem uninhabited. Then, in that fleeting instant when the water of a receding wave flows seaward like a thin stream of liquid glass, there are suddenly hundreds of little gnome-like faces peering through the sandy floor—beady-eyed, long-whiskered faces set in bodies so nearly the color of their background that they can barely be seen. And when, almost instantly, the faces fade back into invisibility, as though a host of strange little troglodytes had momentarily looked out through the curtains of their hidden world and as abruptly retired within it, the illusion is strong that one has seen nothing except in imagination—that there was merely an apparition induced by the magical quality of this world of shifting sand and foaming water.   RACHEL CARSON

ANALYSIS

1. Underline key words in the topic sentence.
2. When arranging details, does Rachel Carson stay strictly with the time order?
3. Point out two effective comparisons.

From THE EDGE OF THE SEA by Rachel Carson. Copyright © 1955. Reprinted by permission of Houghton Mifflin Company.

4. Notice that neither *you* nor *I* appears in the paragraph. An impersonal *one* appears twice. What is the advantage of this point of view?

STRUCTURE FOR STUDY

"It is an extraordinary thing to watch the sand come to life if one happens to be wading where there is a large colony of the crabs."

DICTION

1. What does a *gnome-like face* look like?
2. Define *troglodytes*.
3. In the last sentence, what words might the author have chosen instead of *fade, abruptly retired, shifting, foaming?*

ASSIGNMENT

Write a descriptive paragraph. Be generous with specific details. Some objects for description are suggested below:

1. a tornado
2. a landscape
3. the campus at night
4. the response of an audience

Paragraph 15

When I enter a forest on land, I feel like an intruder, crunching dead twigs and dry leaves underfoot, sending deer and birds into flight. But there is a sense of privilege in descending quietly into a sea forest. If my air tank brushes a frond, it continues to sway, and the inhabitants of a sea forest—from darting perch to rockbound starfish—remain unperturbed. A seal may speed torpedo-like toward me, only to arc away in a playful somersault as if he were bounding off a trampoline. Here I feel tolerated, not resented, free to glide through a wilderness which hides nothing from a visitor.

WESLEY MARX

From KELP FORESTS IN THE PACIFIC by Wesley Marx. *The Atlantic Monthly,* September, 1966. Reprinted by permission of the author.

ANALYSIS

1. Notice the way that Wesley Marx blends description with personal opinion or impressions as he makes a contrast.
2. What does he contrast with twigs, with fleeing deer, with resentment?
3. What do the two forests have in common?

STRUCTURE FOR STUDY

"A seal may speed torpedo-like toward me, only to arc away in a playful somersault as if he were bounding off a trampoline."

DICTION

Point out specific examples of graphic diction; after each give commonplace phraseology that the author did not choose—*crunching dead twigs*, not *stepping on dead branches*, or *only to arc away*, not *just to swim off*, and so forth.

ASSIGNMENT

Write a paragraph of contrast, blending both description and personal experience or opinions. Here are some suggested topics:

1. sailing and flying
2. participant and spectator
3. sightseeing alone and with a tour group

Paragraph 16

The "realist" sees only the surface features of things; he sees the manifest world, he can reproduce it photographically in his mind, and he can act by manipulating things and people as they appear in this picture. The insane person is incapable of seeing reality as it is;

From MAN FOR HIMSELF: AN INQUIRY INTO THE PSYCHOLOGY OF ETHICS by Erich Fromm. Copyright © 1947. Reprinted by permission of Holt, Rinehart and Winston, Inc.

he perceives reality only as a symbol and a reflection of his inner world. Both are sick. The sickness of the psychotic who has lost contact with reality is such that he cannot function socially. The sickness of the "realist" impoverishes him as a human being. While he is not incapacitated in his social functioning, his view of reality is so distorted because of its lack of depth and perspective that he is apt to err when more than manipulation of immediately given data and short-range aims are involved. *"Realism" seems to be the very opposite of insanity and yet it is only its complement.*

ERICH FROMM

ANALYSIS

1. According to Erich Fromm, what does a "realist" see? Why do quotation marks enclose *realist*?
2. What does an insane person see?
3. What is the function of the short third sentence? How does it link ideas?
4. How does the sickness of the insane differ from that of the "realist"?
5. What is the relationship between the second sentence and the last one? Why is the last sentence italicized?

STRUCTURE FOR STUDY

"While he is not incapacitated in his social functioning, his view of reality is so distorted because of its lack of depth and perspective that he is apt to err when more than manipulation of immediately given data and short-range aims are involved."

DICTION

Find synonyms for (1) *psychotic*, (2) *impoverishes*, (3) *incapacitated*, (4) *manipulation*, and (5) *complement*. Be sure that your synonyms would fit the same context.

ASSIGNMENT

Compare two types of people or things that are apparent opposites but are in reality complements. Hold the key idea for the last sentence, and underline this sentence for emphasis. Here are some possible complements:

1. the musician and the mathematician
2. a man and a woman
3. the animate and inanimate

Paragraph 17

I remember one Victoria Day when there was a baseball game between our town and Shaunavon. Alfie Carpenter, from a river-bottom ranch just west of town, was catching for the Whitemud team. He was a boy who had abused me and my kind for years, shoving us off the footbridge, tripping us unexpectedly, giving us the hip, breaking up our hideouts in the brush, stampeding the town herd that was in our charge, and generally making himself lovable. This day I looked up from something just in time to see the batter swing and a foul tip catch Alfie full in the face. For a second he stayed bent over with a hand over his mouth; I saw the blood start in a quick stream through his fingers. My feelings were very badly mixed, for I had dreamed often enough of doing just that to Alfie Carpenter's face, but I was somewhat squeamish about human pain and I couldn't enjoy seeing the dream come true. Moreover I knew with a cold certainty that the ball had hit Alfie at least four times as hard as I had ever imagined hitting him, and there he stood, still on his feet and obviously conscious. A couple of players came up and took his arms and he shook them off, straightened up, spat out a splatter of blood and teeth and picked up his mitt as if to go on with the game. Of course they would not let him—but what a gesture! said my envious and appalled soul. There was a two-tooth hole when Alfie said something; he freed his elbows and swaggered to the side of the field. Watching him, my father broke out in a short, incredulous laugh. "Tough kid!" he said to the man next, and the tone of his voice goose-pimpled me like a breeze on a sweaty skin, for in all my life he had never spoken either to or of me in that voice of approval. Alfie Carpenter, with his broken nose and bloody mouth, was a boy I hated and feared, but most of all I envied his competence to be what his masculine and semibarbarous world said a man should be.   WALLACE STEGNER

From SPECIFICATIONS FOR A HERO by Wallace Stegner. From *Wolf Willow* by Wallace Stegner. Copyright © 1962 by Wallace Stegner. Reprinted by permission of The Viking Press, Inc.

ANALYSIS

1. Briefly point out or outline the plot structure of Wallace Stegner's narrative paragraph: the exposition of setting, situation, and characters; the ascending action; the climax; the ending.
2. What is the point of the narrative?
3. How does this narrative writing differ from the story told in Paragraph 12?
4. How does narration differ from description (see Paragraph 14) and from exposition (see Paragraph 1)?

STRUCTURE FOR STUDY

"'Tough kid!' he said to the man next, and the tone of his voice goose-pimpled me like a breeze on a sweaty skin, for in all my life he had never spoken either to or of me in that voice of approval."

DICTION

1. Select at least five words that you think are especially well chosen.
2. Define in context *incredulous* and *appalled.*
3. Find narrative details that could not be deleted without impairing the effect of the story.

ASSIGNMENT

Using Paragraph 17 as a model, write a narrative selected from your own personal experiences. Or if you wish, create a story putting yourself in as a main character. Use the I-was-there approach. Establish your setting and conflict and introduce main characters early so that the main part of the paragraph will deal with action.

Capital punishment is, in my opinion, morally wrong. It has a bad effect on everyone, especially those involved in it. It gives a false sense of security to the public. It is vastly expensive. Worst of all it beclouds the entire issue of motivation in crime, which is so importantly relevant to the question of what to do for and with the criminal that will be most constructive to society as a whole. Punishing—and even killing—criminals may yield a kind of grim gratification; let us all admit that there are times when we are so shocked at the depredations of an offender that we persuade ourselves that this is a man the Creator didn't intend to create, and that we had better help correct the mistake. But playing God in this way has no conceivable moral or scientific justification.   KARL MENNINGER

ANALYSIS

1. Notice that Karl Menninger first states briefly and clearly his definite stand on a controversial issue.
2. How do the next four sentences support his side of the argument? How are these sentences linked and arranged?
3. Why does the author shift his point of view in the sixth sentence?
4. Explain why the last sentence is or is not a clincher.

STRUCTURE FOR STUDY

"Punishing—and even killing—criminals may yield a kind of grim gratification; let us all admit that there are times when we are so shocked at the depredations of an offender that we persuade ourselves that this is a man the Creator didn't intend to create, and that we had better help correct the mistake."

DICTION

What is the meaning in context of (1) *relevant* and (2) *depredations?*

From VERDICT GUILTY—NOW WHAT? by Karl Menninger. *Harper's Magazine,* August, 1959. Copyright © 1959 by Harper & Brothers. Reprinted by permission of the author.

ASSIGNMENT

Write a paragraph presenting an argument. First state your position; then give reasons, in order of importance, why your side of the argument is the right side. Next present the most popular opinion of the opposing side in order to attack it. Write a strong last sentence. The following is a list of controversial questions, one of which you may choose as a springboard for your argument.

1. Is euthanasia morally wrong?
2. Should communes replace family units?
3. Are our universities meeting the needs of students?
4. Should we fight our wars with mercenaries or with draftees?
5. Is an apocalypse approaching?

Paragraph 19

Epigrams can be concocted more mechanically than other satiric devices. One method consists of changing a cliché slightly, so that an incongruous effect is produced. (Huxley: "And while there is death, there is hope." Twain: "All the modern inconveniences.") Another way is the coining of a cynical definition. (Mencken: "Conscience: the inner voice which warns us that someone is looking." Bierce: "Diaphragm: a muscular partition separating the disorders of the chest from disorders of the bowels.") A third method is stating pungently a belief widely held but rarely expressed. (Proverb: "Poverty is not a sin, but it's a great deal worse.") A variation of this method is a new way of stating an old idea. (Mencken: "Man weeps to think that he will die so soon; woman, that she was born so long ago.") And a fourth, the most difficult, is a polished statement of an original idea, as in Montaigne, Confucius, Nietzsche, Shaw, La Rochefoucauld, Shakespeare, Emerson, Schopenhauer, and Bacon. (Thoreau: "The mass of men lead lives of quiet desperation.") All of these methods rely on balanced construction and economy of words.

LEONARD FEINBERG

From INTRODUCTION TO SATIRE by Leonard Feinberg. © 1967 by The Iowa State University Press, Ames, Iowa. Reprinted by permission.

ANALYSIS

1. Study the organization, the parallel structures, and the arrangement of ideas in Paragraph 19.
2. Relate the first sentence to the last one.
3. What four classifications are presented?
4. How is each satiric method explained?
5. Why do you suppose Leonard Feinberg decided to use numerous parentheses and colons?

STRUCTURE FOR STUDY

"A third method is stating pungently a belief widely held but rarely expressed. (Proverb: 'Poverty is not a sin, but it's a great deal worse.')"

DICTION

Explain the meaning in context of (1) *concocted*, (2) *satiric*, (3) *cliché*, (4) *incongruous*, (5) *cynical*, (6) *pungently*, and (7) *economy*.

ASSIGNMENT

Using Paragraph 19 as a model, develop an idea by way of classification; supply a specific example to illustrate each classification. For transition use these sentence beginnings: *One . . . . Another . . . . A third . . . . And a fourth . . . .* Write a clincher sentence beginning with *All . . . .* Some suggested topics are:

1. Four kinds of students are voicing their opinions on this current issue.
2. Household truisms usually fall into one of four categories.
3. Four kinds of slogans appeal to the emotions.

Empathy occurs in the moment one human being speaks with another. It is impossible to understand another individual if it is impossible at the same time to identify oneself with him. Drama is the artistic expression of empathy. Other examples of empathy are those cases in which someone has a strange feeling of uneasiness when he notices another in danger. This empathy may be so strong that one makes involuntary defense movements, even though there is no danger to oneself. We all know the well-known gesture which is made when someone has dropped his glass! At a bowling alley one may see certain players following the course of the ball with movements of their body as though they wanted to influence its course by this movement! Similarly during football games whole sections of people in the grandstand will push in the direction of their favorite team, or make resistive pressure when the opponent team has the ball. A common expression is the involuntary application of imaginary brakes by the occupants of a motor car whenever they feel that they are in danger. Few people can pass a tall building in which someone is washing a window without experiencing certain contractions and defense movements. When a speaker loses his presence of mind and cannot proceed, people in the audience are oppressed and uneasy. In the theatre particularly we can hardly avoid identifying ourselves with the players, or prevent ourselves from acting the most varied roles within ourselves. Our entire life is very much dependent upon the faculty of identification. If we seek for the origin of this ability to act and feel as if we were someone else, we can find it in the existence of an inborn social feeling. This is, as a matter of fact, a cosmic feeling and a reflection of the connectedness of the whole cosmos which lives in us; it is an inescapable characteristic of being a human being. It gives us the faculty of identifying ourselves with things which are quite outside our own body.　　ALFRED ADLER

ANALYSIS

1. Study Alfred Adler's treatment of empathy; notice that he defines by explaining, illustrating, and analyzing.
2. Of the examples given, which ones do you think most clearly illustrate empathy?

3. What synonym for *empathy* or *empathize* appears repeatedly?
4. Summarize the last four sentences, and relate this summary to the second sentence of the paragraph.

STRUCTURE FOR STUDY

"At a bowling alley one may see certain players following the course of the ball with movements of their body as though they wanted to influence its course by this movement!"

DICTION

What does Adler mean by (1) *involuntary defense movements,* (2) *resistive pressure,* (3) *experiencing certain contractions,* (4) *the faculty of identification,* and (5) *a cosmic feeling?*

ASSIGNMENT

Using Paragraph 20 as a model, explain a word by (1) naming an exact synonym, (2) providing at least five detailed examples, and (3) pointing out its significance in our lives. You may wish to explain one of the words listed below.

1.	marriage	6.	ESP
2.	self-education	7.	hell
3.	ambition	8.	NOW*
4.	rapport	9.	ecumenism
5.	discrimination	10.	abortion

---

* National Organization for Women.

Varieties of Compositions

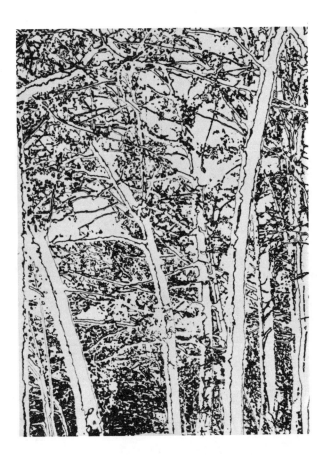

A word of explanation

Part 3 is not "a reader." It is rather "a writer," a group of short modern articles selected to serve as practical models for the type of writing often required in college, both in English classes and in other courses.

When taking essay-type tests in many college classes, you often have little or no choice of the kind of writing you are to do. That is, the discussion questions themselves ordinarily designate what type of composition is expected. Such questions begin with *Define, Describe, Analyze, Explain the process of.* A study of the varieties of compositions in this section should help you develop a special know-how as a test-taker.

In freshman English class, however, you will probably have chances to decide upon a type of writing. You may be asked to write on a particular subject, perhaps the battle of the sexes, the problem of crime or drugs, a social issue, or a political crisis. But you are often free to decide whether you will express an opinion or present an argument, or prepare a description or an analysis. Once you have a subject, you are like an artist with a small canvas who wants to paint a landscape. Because of the limitation of space, you, like the artist, must decide not only what to include but also what to leave out.

To make wise decisions, you should define your purpose. Remember that most writing is communication, that at least two persons are normally involved: the writer and a reader. When selecting material to communicate, you as the writer should keep your reader firmly in mind; ask yourself such questions as: What effect do I want to have on my reader? Shall I try to inform him? persuade him? entertain him? Answering these questions can help you establish a purpose. Then you may select and arrange your ideas effectively.

The purpose of exposition is to inform by explaining. The aim of argument is to persuade, not merely to inform. The goal of description is to make a reader see. The purpose of narration varies: some stories amuse; others teach; still others mystify or frighten. These four types of writing are often combined to achieve a given purpose. Whether using one type or a combination, you should decide upon the method of composition that best suits your aim.

Sharing a personal experience

Compositions based on personal experiences do more than express what writers think or believe. When you share a personal experience, you may tell of what you did (an incident), what you saw (an observation), what you heard (a report or a dialogue), what you felt (an impression), what you dreamed (a fantasy), what you remember (a memory)— or a combination of any of these. As you read the next four selections describing personal experiences, notice the range of content.

A Tire Kicker on the Prowl
Loudon Wainwright

Of course, from time to time one must stop looking and buy 1
a car, and there is no worse moment for me. I come to the engagement with the certain feeling that I am going to make a terrible deal, that the salesman will trick me, that the car itself will be a disastrous lemon.

It all starts with the prices, and the varying possibilities here 2
throw me into a profound confusion. To begin with, I know that the price at the bottom of the list on the car's window can be negotiated downward, and the chance I will blow this negotiation makes me sweat. The salesman's invitation to sit down with

From A TIRE KICKER ON THE PROWL by Loudon Wainwright. *Life* Magazine, April 14, 1967. © 1967 Time Inc.

him at his little desk is a signal for near panic, and I try desperately to keep up with his mysterious mathematics by adding upside down as he scratches on his pad.

The whole business of trading-in ruinously compounds the problem. When the agent in charge of setting a price on my old car goes into action, I can hardly bear to watch. He prowls the car suspiciously, slams the doors too hard, gets inside and starts the engine with contemptuous familiarity. Then he gets out, stands back and looks at the car in brooding distaste, like a man who has stumbled on a decaying body in a swamp. His trade-in price, when he finally grumbles it, is delivered as if he were doing me the most immense imaginable favor to put any cash value on the automobile at all. At this point in buying a new car, I am stricken with a sudden, irrational loyalty for the old one, but this fierce loyalty can be dissipated by any salesman clever enough to offer me a reasonable increase—say $25. 3

Unfortunately, I have a good friend who knows a lot about cars and takes great pleasure in dispensing advice about how to buy them. "That new Ripper Rabbit wagon is a great car," he'll say to me. "Just get that with the limited schlocks, the graphinated sliding and zip-out muffler and you'll have the best little buy in America." So I read a list of these accessories to the salesman and he says: "Oh, you want the graphinated sliding, do you? Not many people ask for that. Actually we don't make that in our Fast River plant. That calls for a little adjustment in these figures. . . ." And when I tell my friend the final price of the car, he coolly tells me that if I hadn't got so impatient, I could have got the same model for $300 less through this dealer he knows in the next town. 4

QUESTIONS

1. What controlling idea is stated in Paragraph 1? Are all of Loudon Wainwright's fears common, or are they all unique?
2. In Paragraph 2, is the situation routine or exaggerated? Explain your answer.
3. What is the order of the details in Paragraph 3? Point out several examples of effective diction and one striking comparison.
4. How in Paragraph 4 do the direct quotations relate to the controlling idea? Why does the author not begin a new paragraph with a change of speaker? At the end of the last quotation, why are four periods better than one?

(1) a *profound* confusion, (2) with *contemptuous* familiarity, (3) *fierce* loyalty can be *dissipated*, (4) limited *schlocks*.

FROM

Travels with Charley

John Steinbeck

About fifty yards away two coyotes stood watching me, their   1
tawny coats blending with sand and sun. I knew that with any
quick or suspicious movement of mine they could drift into invisibility. With the most casual slowness I reached down my
new rifle from its sling over my bed—the .222 with its bitter
little high-speed, long-range stings. Very slowly I brought the
rifle up. Perhaps in the shade of my house I was half hidden by
the blinding light outside. The little rifle has a beautiful telescope sight with a wide field. The coyotes had not moved.

I got both of them in the field of my telescope, and the glass   2
brought them very close. Their tongues lolled out so that they
seemed to smile mockingly. They were favored animals, not
starved, but well furred, the golden hair tempered with black
guard hairs. Their little lemon-yellow eyes were plainly visible
in the glass. I moved the cross hairs to the breast of the right-
hand animal, and pushed the safety. My elbows on the table
steadied the gun. The cross hairs lay unmoving on the brisket.
And then the coyote sat down like a dog and its right rear paw
came up to scratch the right shoulder.

My finger was reluctant to touch the trigger. I must be get-   3
ting very old and my ancient conditioning worn thin. Coyotes
are vermin. They steal chickens. They thin the ranks of quail and
all other game birds. They must be killed. They are the enemy.
My first shot would drop the sitting beast, and the other would
whirl to fade away. I might very well pull him down with a
running shot because I am a good rifleman.

And I did not fire. My training said, "Shoot!" and my age re-   4
plied, "There isn't a chicken within thirty miles, and if there are
any they aren't my chickens. And this waterless place is not quail

country. No, these boys are keeping their figures with kangaroo rats and jackrabbits, and that's vermin eat vermin. Why should I interfere?"

"Kill them," my training said. "Everyone kills them. It's a 5 public service." My finger moved to the trigger. The cross was steady on the breast just below the panting tongue. I could imagine the splash and jar of angry steel, the leap and struggle until the torn heart failed, and then, not too long later, the shadow of a buzzard, and another. By that time I would be long gone— out of the desert and across the Colorado River. And beside the sagebrush there would be a naked, eyeless skull, a few picked bones, a spot of black dried blood and a few rags of golden fur.

I guess I'm too old and too lazy to be a good citizen. The 6 second coyote stood sidewise to my rifle. I moved the cross hairs to his shoulder and held steady. There was no question of missing with that rifle at that range. I owned both animals. Their lives were mine. I put the safety on and laid the rifle on the table. Without the telescope they were not so intimately close. The hot blast of light tousled the air to shimmering.

Then I remembered something I heard long ago that I hope 7 is true. It was unwritten law in China, so my informant told me, that when one man saved another's life he became responsible for that life to the end of its existence. For, having interfered with a course of events, the savior could not escape his responsibility. And that has always made good sense to me.

Now I had a token responsibility for two live and healthy 8 coyotes. In the delicate world of relationships, we are tied together for all time. I opened two cans of dog food and left them as a votive.

QUESTIONS

1. What setting, situation, and problem are presented in Paragraph 1?
2. Point out narrative details in Paragraph 2 that anticipate Steinbeck's failure to pull the trigger.
3. Did you notice the contrasting arguments in Paragraphs 3 and 4? Are they realistic? Why or why not?
4. Does the author base his decision not to kill on logical reasons, on the imagined sequence of events, on both of these, or on neither? Explain your answer.
5. Do the last three paragraphs surprise the reader? What does the last line mean? Why do you suppose Steinbeck decided to share this experience?

WORD STUDY

(1) the .222 with its *bitter* little high-speed, long-range stings, (2) the golden hair *tempered* with black guard hairs, (3) the *splash* and *jar* of *angry* steel, (4) a few *rags* of golden fur, (5) *hot blast of light tousled* the air to *shimmering.*

A Discharge of Electricity

Paul Horgan

During lunch one day a particularly violent thunderstorm broke over us almost without warning.

I made a move.

My father said sternly,

"Richard!"

Thunder and lightning seemed to spring at us from the very trees at our door.

Fear drove me from the table in spite of the commands of my father. I ran to hide with my heart beating out the ejaculatory prayers of safety. "My Jesus, mercy!" said my bones at every house-cracking crash.

In a few moments the door of my closet was pulled open. My mother was there, wearing her heavy stiff yellow raincoat and holding my smaller one.

"Richard? Come?"

"No!"

"Come with me, my darling. *Schnell?* Come?"

Her voice was sharp and commanding. She reached for my arm and pulled me from the closet and held out my sou'wester. "Put this on! Quick!"

The storm was making the house cry in its wooden ribs.

"No! No!"

She slapped me hard on the cheek, which she had never done before. Appalled by shock, I put on my raincoat. She took my arm and led me to the porch.

"Where are we going?"

"We are going to meet the storm, not run away from it."

"No!"

Sharing a Personal Experience   **149**

She took me down the steps, down the island slope, down to the dock, down to the far end of the dock where there was no refuge—where there was much actual danger from lightning bolts. We were soaked through in a second, for the wind tore at our raincoats. The lake danced wildly with waves. The far shore was lost except when the lightning flashed over there and here above us and everywhere. Calling to me above the wind, my mother said,

"Richard, look!" She shook me and pointed to the wild sky, the sweeps of rain on the lake, and then at the tearing strikes of lightning amidst the clouds. "Richard! Look! Why be afraid? *It is so beautiful!*"

She put her arm about my shoulders and when the lightning struck I could feel how she too trembled before the power of God. But how new was her idea that this power was beautiful! I stared at the new idea as I stared at a world I had never been able to see before. I met an entirely fresh way to regard the thing that had terrorized my childhood. About to be convinced, I shouted,

"But it's dangerous!"

"Of course it's dangerous," she replied. The wind tried to hollow out her words and sweep them away, but I heard her meaning even so. "There is something dangerous about all beauty, and it is still beautiful! I don't know what it is, but—."

We stood there and the thunder and lightning broke over us, here, and afar, and my vision cleared, and I knew that what she said was true. After the great gift of life itself, it was the finest gift she made me, this means of losing fear. In immediate terms, then, and afterward, any storm was charged, for me, as much with beauty as with danger.

QUESTIONS

1. From what point of view is "A Discharge of Electricity" told? How do vocabulary, sentence structure, and details show that the writer is grown rather than a child? How would the personal experience be changed if the mother, a strong-willed woman of German descent, were the narrator?

2. Do you agree with the statement: "There is something dangerous about all beauty"? Name specific examples (like Helen of Troy or a rose amid thorns) to support Horgan's statement. Can you name exceptions?

3. Does the reader of "A Discharge of Electricity" identify with or sympathize with the writer? Why or why not?
4. How does Horgan's experience relate to the title of the book in which this selection originally appeared—*Things As They Are?*
5. How significant is the dialogue? What effect would changing direct quotations to summary statements or to indirect quotations have?

WORD STUDY

(1) the *ejaculatory* prayers of safety, (2) the *tearing strikes* of lightning, (3) any storm was *charged* . . . with beauty . . . with danger.

---

n the Jungle
William Styron

On Tuesday night I left a party on the Near North Side with a friend, whom I shall call Jason Epstein, in order to see what was going on in nearby Lincoln Park. There had been rumors of some sort of demonstration and when we arrived, at a little before midnight, we saw that in fact a group of young people had gathered there—I estimated 1,000 or so—most of them sitting peacefully on the grass in the dark, illuminated dimly by the light of a single portable floodlamp, and fanning out in a semi-circle beneath a ten-foot-high wooden cross. The previous night, testing the 11 P.M. curfew, several thousands had assembled in the park and had been brutally routed by the police who bloodied dozens of demonstrators. Tonight the gathering was a sort of coalition between the yippies and the followers of a group of Near North Side clergymen, who had organized the sit-in in order to claim the right of the people of the neighborhood to use the park without police harassment. "This is our park!" one minister proclaimed over the loudspeaker. "We will not be moved!" Someone was playing a guitar and folk songs were sung; there was considerable restlessness and tension in the air, even though it was hard to believe that the police would actually attack this tranquil assembly which so resembled a Presbyterian prayer meeting rather than any group threatening public de-

1

corum and order. Yet in the black sky a helicopter wheeled over us in a watchful ellipse, and word got back to us that the police had indeed formed ranks several hundred yards down the slope to the east, beyond our sight. A few people began to leave and the chant went up: "Sit down! Sit down!" Most of us remained seated and part of the crowd began singing "The Battle Hymn of the Republic." Meanwhile, instructions were being given out by the old campaigners: don't panic, if forced to the street stay away from the walls and blind alleys, if knocked to the ground use your jacket as a cushion against clubs, above all walk, don't run. The time was now about twelve-thirty. Vaseline was offered as a protection against MACE, wet strips of cloth were handed out to muffle the tear gas. The tension was not very pleasant; while it is easy to over-dramatize such a moment, it does contain its element of raw threat, a queasy, visceral suspense that can only be compared to certain remembered episodes during combat training. "They'll be here in two minutes!" the minister announced.

And suddenly they were here, coming over the brow of the 2 slope fifty yards away, a truly stupefying sight—one hundred or more of the police in a phalanx abreast, clubs at the ready, in helmets and gas masks, just behind them a huge perambulating machine with nozzles, like the type used for spraying insecticide, disgorging clouds of yellowish gas, the whole advancing panoply illuminated by batteries of mobile floodlights. Because of the smoke, and the great cross outlined against it, yet also because of the helmeted and masked figures—resembling nothing so much as those rubberized wind-up automata from a child's playbox of horrors—I had a quick sense of the medieval in juxtaposition with the twenty-first century or, more exactly, a kind of science fiction fantasy, as if a band of primitive Christians on another planet had suddenly found themselves set upon by mechanized legions from Jupiter.

Certainly, whatever the exact metaphor it summoned up, the 3 sight seemed to presage the shape of the world to come, but by now we were up, all of us, off and away—not running, *walking*, fast—toward Clark Street, bleeding tears from the gas. The streets next to the park became a madhouse. The police had not been content to run us out of the park but, charging from the opposite direction, had flanked us, and were harrying people down the streets and up alleys. On a traffic island in the middle of Clark Street a young man was knocked to his knees and beaten senseless. Unsuspecting motorists, caught up in the pandemonium, began to collide with one another up and down the street. The crowd wailed with alarm and split into fragments. I heard the sound of splintering glass as a stone went through the windshield of a police car. Then somehow we disengaged ourselves from the center of the crowd and made our way down Wells Street, relatively deserted where in the dingy nightclubs Go-Go girls oblivious to the rout outside calmly wiggled their asses in silhouette against crimson windows.

QUESTIONS

1. In Paragraph 1, how does William Styron combine what he sees, remembers, hears, and thinks? How does this account differ from a news report of the same event?
2. How does the I-was-there approach affect the description in Paragraph 2? Why do the comparisons evoke more horror than do the vividly factual details?
3. How does Styron make a transition from Paragraph 2 to Paragraph 3? What word groups best capture the sights and sounds of the "madhouse"?
4. What are the implications of the last sentence?

WORD STUDY

(1) public *decorum*, (2) in a watchful *ellipse*, (3) a queasy, *visceral* suspense, (4) a huge *perambulating* machine, (5) the whole advancing *panoply*, (6) the medieval in *juxtaposition* with the twenty-first century, (7) the exact *metaphor* it summoned up, (8) seemed to *presage* the shape, (9) were *harrying* people, (10) Go-Go girls *oblivious* to the *rout* outside.

SUGGESTIONS FOR WRITING

1. Share a personal experience similar to that of Loudon Wainwright's tire kicker, an experience with which many readers can easily identify. State the setting, situation, and problem in the first paragraph; then plunge immediately into action and narrative details. Arrange material chronologically, using such transitional words as *first, later, soon, then, finally.*

154   Varieties of Compositions

Suggested controlling ideas:

    a. I do not feel at home in the East (West, South, or North).

    b. I cannot break my smoking habit.

    c. I was meeting strangers in a crowded airport.

2. Write a composition like Paul Horgan's "Discharge of Electricity," which relates an unusual childhood experience. Start with action, and use dialogue to advance the story.

    Suggested endings:

    a. I had gained a new insight.

    b. I had discovered an unexpected side of an old friend.

    c. I had learned to laugh at my own limitations.

3. Use Steinbeck's selection from *Travels with Charley* as a model for a personal-experience composition. As you relate your thoughts, create suspense and work toward a surprise ending. Be generous with descriptive and narrative details.

    Suggested beginnings:

    a. Investigating the noise just outside my bedroom window, I flashed a beam of light toward the dark shrubbery.

    b. Holding a hamburger in one hand and straightening out a road map with the other, I glanced up to see a stranger's eyes in my rearview mirror.

4. Write about a newsworthy event similar to Styron's account from "In the Jungle." Use vivid factual details and striking comparisons that especially suit an I-was-there approach. If you have not been an eyewitness to such excitement, then select an interesting newspaper article and imagine the events as if you were on the scene.

    Suggested topics:

    a. a happening on campus

    b. a Fourth of July highway statistic

    c. as the fire (storm, battle) raged

5. Use the photograph on page 154 as a springboard for a composition on the "Generation Gap." Perhaps your personal experiences link you with the young man sitting on the step. Or, if you have had to cope with those younger than yourself, you may be more closely related to the passer-by.

Expressing an opinion

As you read the next three selections, notice that each author shares an opinion, his point of view. His mood is not argumentative. You are comfortably free to agree or to disagree—or to express a wholly different opinion in a composition of your own. See the Suggestions for Writing that end this chapter.

The Return of Nature

Eric Hoffer

All through adult life I had a feeling of revulsion when   1
told how nature aids and guides us, how like a stern mother she
nudges and pushes man to fulfill her wise designs. As a migratory
worker from the age of eighteen I knew nature as ill-disposed
and inhospitable. If I stretched on the ground to rest, nature
pushed its hard knuckles into my sides, and sent bugs, burs, and
foxtails to make me get up and be gone. As a placer miner I had
to run the gauntlet of buckbrush, manzanita, and poison oak when
I left the road to find my way to a creek. Direct contact with nature almost always meant scratches, bites, torn clothes, and grime
that ate its way into every pore of the body. To make life bearable
I had to interpose a protective layer between myself and nature.
On the paved road, even when miles from anywhere, I felt at

home. I had a sense of kinship with the winding, endless road that cares not where it goes and what its load.

Almost all the books I read spoke worshipfully of nature. Nature was pure, innocent, serene, health-giving, bountiful, the fountainhead of elevated thoughts and noble feelings. It seemed that every writer was a "nature boy." I assumed that these people had no share in the world's work, and did not know nature at close quarters. It also seemed to me that they had a grievance. For coupled with their admiration of nature was a distaste for man and man's work. Man was a violator, a defiler and deformer. 2

The truth about nature I found in the newspapers, in the almost daily reports of floods, tornados, blizzards, hurricanes, typhoons, hailstorms, sandstorms, earthquakes, avalanches, eruptions, inundations, pests, plagues, and famines. Sometimes when reading about nature's terrible visitations and her massacre of the innocents it seemed to me that we are surrounded by devouring, pitiless forces, that the earth was full of anger, the sky dark with wrath, and that man had built the city as a refuge from a hostile, nonhuman cosmos. I realized that the contest between man and nature has been the central drama of the universe. 3

Man became what he is not with the aid, but in spite, of nature. Humanization meant breaking away from nature, getting out from underneath the iron necessities which dominate nature. By the same token, dehumanization means the reclamation of man by nature. It means the return of nature. It is significant that humanization had its start in the fact that man was an unfinished, defective animal. Nature dealt niggardly with him from the beginning. It brought him forth naked and helpless, without inborn skills, and without specialized organs to serve him as weapons and tools. Unlike other animals, man was not a born technician with a built-in tool kit. Small wonder that for millennia man worshiped animals, nature's more favored children. Yet this misbegotten creature has made himself lord of the globe. He has evolved fabulous substitutes for the instincts and the specialized organs that he lacked, and rather than adjust himself to the world he has changed the world to fit him. This, surely, is the supreme miracle. If history is to have meaning it must be the history of humanization, of man's tortuous ascent through the ages, of his ceaseless effort to break away from the rest of creation and become an order apart. 4

QUESTIONS

1. What key words in the first and second sentences give the controlling idea of "The Return of Nature"?
2. What specific reasons does Eric Hoffer present to support his opinion?
3. How is a paved road related to the author's opinion of nature? Is the road a symbol?
4. In Paragraphs 2 and 3, what contrast is given? Which paragraph is the stronger of the two? Why is it stronger?
5. In Paragraph 4, how is *humanization* defined? What does Hoffer mean by *dehumanization*?

WORD STUDY

(1) Man was a *violator,* a *defiler* and *deformer,* (2) Nature dealt *niggardly,* (3) man's *tortuous* ascent.

Motorcar: The Mechanical Bride
Marshall McLuhan

To mistake the car for a status symbol, just because it is asked to be taken as anything but a car, is to mistake the whole meaning of this very late product of the mechanical age that is now yielding its form to electric technology. The car is a superb piece of uniform, standardized mechanism that is of a piece with the Gutenberg technology and literacy which created the first classless society in the world. The car gave to the democratic cavalier his horse and armor and haughty insolence in one package, transmogrifying the knight into a misguided missile. In fact, the American car did not level downward, but upward, toward the aristocratic idea. Enormous increase and distribution of power had also been the equalizing force of literacy and various other forms of mechanization. The willingness to accept the car as a status symbol, restricting its more expansive form to the use of higher executives, is not a mark of the car and mechanical age, but of the electric forces that are now ending this mechanical age of uniformity and standardization, and recreating the norms of status and role.

When the motorcar was new, it exercised the typical mechanical pressure of explosion and separation of functions. It broke up family life, or so it seemed, in the 1920s. It separated work and domicile, as never before. It exploded each city into a dozen suburbs, and then extended many of the forms of urban life along the highways until the open road seemed to become non-stop cities. It created the asphalt jungles, and caused 40,000 square miles of green and pleasant land to be cemented over. With the arrival of plane travel, the motorcar and truck teamed up together to wreck the railways. Today small children plead for a train ride as if it were a stagecoach or horse and cutter: "Before they're *gone*, Daddy." 2

The motorcar ended the countryside and substituted a new landscape in which the car was a sort of steeplechaser. At the same time, the motor destroyed the city as a casual environment in which families could be reared. Streets, and even sidewalks, became too intense a scene for the casual interplay of growing up. As the city filled with mobile strangers, even next-door neighbors became strangers. This is the story of the motorcar, and it has not much longer to run. The tide of taste and tolerance has turned, since TV, to make the hot-car medium increasingly tiresome. Witness the portent of the crosswalk, where the small child has power to stop a cement truck. The same change has rendered the big city unbearable to many who would no more have felt that way ten years ago than they could have enjoyed reading *MAD*. 3

The continuing power of the car medium to transform the patterns of settlement appears fully in the way in which the new urban kitchen has taken on the same central and multiple social character as the old farm kitchen. The farm kitchen had been the key point of entry to the farmhouse, and had become the social center, as well. The new suburban home again makes the kitchen the center and, ideally, is localized for access to and from the car. The car has become the carapace, the protective and aggressive shell, of urban and suburban man. Even before the Volkswagen, observers about street level have often noticed the near-resemblance of cars to shiny-backed insects. In the age of the tactile-oriented skin-diver, this hard shiny carapace is one of the blackest marks against the motorcar. It is for motorized man that the shopping plazas have emerged. They are strange islands that make the pedestrian feel friendless and disembodied. The car bugs him. 4

The car, in a word, has quite refashioned all of the spaces   5
that unite and separate men, and it will continue to do so for a
decade more, by which time the electronic successors to the
car will be manifest.

QUESTIONS

1. What personal opinion is the controlling idea of the whole selection? Where does Marshall McLuhan summarize this opinion?
2. According to Marshall McLuhan, what is the relationship of the motorcar (a) to democracy, (b) to "Gutenberg technology," and (c) to an urban kitchen?
3. What reasons does the author give for this opinion: "The tide of taste and tolerance has turned, since TV, to make the hot-car medium increasingly tiresome."

WORD STUDY

(1) *transmogrifying* the knight, (2) the car was a sort of *steeplechaser*, (3) too *intense* a scene for the *casual interplay* of growing up, (4) the *carapace*, the *protective and aggressive* shell, (5) the age of the *tactile-oriented skin-diver*.

A Charade of Power

Kenneth B. Clark

The dilemma of the Negro, especially of the black college   1
student, in these turbulent days is full of irony and paradox. His
dilemma is compounded by the appearance of change in American institutions, particularly education, and his need to respond
appropriately in terms of the degree of reality of this change. He
often finds that change is an illusion, that he is presented with,
and seems sometimes to invite, merely new forms of racism, in
new guises but, in the end, made of the same stuff.

From A CHARADE OF POWER: BLACK STUDENTS AT WHITE COLLEGES by Kenneth B.
Clark. *The Antioch Review*, Volume XXIX, Number 2 (Summer 1969). Reprinted
by permission of the author and *The Antioch Review*.

His dilemma is rooted in one dominant fact: however noisy   2
his rhetoric, however flamboyant the manifestations of his protest, he is still the minority. Even his "victories" are guided and
permitted by the majority. The armed black students at Cornell
had no real power—not they, but the white majority were in
control. The fact that the white administration and faculty chose
not to act violently in response, but rather to acquiesce—or appear to acquiesce—to demands, did not obscure the evidence of
real power. The guns at the ready were a charade; they were
permitted only because the majority understood they could be
put down whenever it wished to do so. To the extent that whites
encourage in blacks acceptance of this pretense of power, they
are participating in but one more manifestation of an old racism.

Negroes have had centuries of experience of benevolent   3
racism that permits bizarre behavior on the grounds that the
Negro is going through a phase that will be outgrown. Whites
believe this now—and often state it candidly. Black separatism,
particularly among the young, is seen as racially adolescent
behavior, to be understood, tolerated, and even condoned as long
as it does not threaten the real sources of authority. That many
black students do not grasp the pervasive and subtle forms of
white racism is clear in their exultant reaction after "non-negotiable" demands lead to apparent concessions. They believe that
Black Studies Institutes, separate from the governance of the
university, free from the regulations of faculty or degree requirements, or black dormitories from which whites are "excluded,"
are evidence of surrender of majority power. But whites have not
given up, thereby, anything other than the requirement of persistent confrontation with blacks on a basis of black equality.
Negro students miss the fact that voluntary surrender of "power"
by those who hold it is seldom loss of actual power. Symbolic
power may be tendered, however, particularly when those in
authority perceive that negotiators will be satisfied with the mere
appearance of power, indeed, that in some complex way, they
may prefer not to take the risk of competing for the responsibility
of genuine power. Those in power seldom give up more than is
necessary to restore stability—for stability is essential to their
orderly exercise of authority.

If a mayor can buy peace by strategic patronage (no less   4
patronage when black militants rather than old-fashioned wardheelers demand it), he will do so. He need not transform the
ghetto into a viable community if this is not the non-negotiable
demand. If a white-dominated Board of Education can appease
militants, and simultaneously strengthen top quality white-
segregated schools, it need not insist on basic reorganization of

the system. If a national political leader can ease the pressure by offers of subsidies to a few black capitalists, he need not move to abolish poverty, among both Negroes and whites. If a university administration can restore harmony and the image of innovation by a no-strings-attached financial grant to a separate black studies program that may cover a few salaries or subsidize a gas station, it need not move to transform itself into a genuinely nonracial institution dedicated to developing human beings and to helping them develop effective strategies for fundamental social change. No more power is granted than it is necessary to yield.

QUESTIONS

1. What specific details in Paragraph 1 clarify what Clark means by the "dilemma of the Negro"? What is ironic and paradoxical about this dilemma?
2. What is the controlling idea of Paragraph 2? How is Paragraph 2 related to Paragraph 1? to the title?
3. What examples does Clark choose to explain his main point in Paragraph 2? in Paragraph 3? Can you think of other examples that might have been added?
4. What sentences have parallel structures in Paragraph 4? How are they arranged? Why do you suppose Clark did not decide to end the paragraph with another long sentence beginning with *If*?

WORD STUDY

(1) however *flamboyant* the manifestations of his protest, (2) appear to *acquiesce*, (3) guns at the *ready*, (4) experience of *benevolent racism*, (5) the *pervasive* and *subtle* forms of white racism, (6) *Symbolic* power, (7) can buy peace by *strategic patronage*, (8) old-fashioned *wardheelers*, (9) a *viable* community, (10) A *Charade* of Power.

SUGGESTIONS FOR WRITING

1. Using the approach of Eric Hoffer in "The Return of Nature," write a composition giving reasons for a personal opinion. *Suggested organization:* In Paragraph 1, clearly state your opinion, clarifying it with specific details drawn from personal experience. In Paragraph 2, give an opposing opinion. In Paragraph 3, present

Syd Greenberg, DPI

your own observations to contradict ideas in Paragraph 2. Finally, write a concluding paragraph showing the significance of your views. Throughout your composition, aim for a clear expression of your opinion: have a this-is-what-I-believe attitude rather than a this-is-what-you-should-believe stance.

Suggested central ideas:

    a. The realists I know are not pessimists.

    b. No American today is merely a number.

    c. I cannot relate to Ernest Hemingway's characters.

2. Use Marshall McLuhan's "Motorcar: The Mechanical Bride" as a model for a composition. Start with a statement of opinion, preferably an unusual point of view, to gain the interest of your reader. Use specific details to explain your main ideas. Summarize your views in a short concluding paragraph.

Suggested beginnings:

    a. A college degree, a yacht, a home in the country, a trip around the world—these status symbols died in the sixties.

    b. Those who talk most about "the generation gap" do not even know what it means.

3. After reviewing "A Charade of Power," write a composition giving your opinion of a condition or situation on your own college campus. Select a topic of current interest.

4. Write a composition answering this question: *Who is to blame for pollution?* You may name one group or single out three or four groups that you believe bear heavy responsibility. Give reasons to justify your choices.

Writing a description

Description presents a word picture. You may describe whatever you look upon—anything, say, from a sick child to a heavyweight champion, from a gyroscope to a computer. You may choose to describe action or still life, what you see in reality or in your imagination.

Whoever or whatever you describe, you need to have a purpose. This purpose should not only affect your selection of details but also shape your organization. Like other types of writing, description may entertain, inform, or persuade. Your description may be subjective, presented in first person (*I, me, we*) and interspersed with personal reactions. Or it may be objective, using an impersonal third-person point of view (*it, they, one*). Remember that when personal opinions or experiences, definitions, or analyses appear in a descriptive essay they are incidental or subordinate rather than predominant.

No Pocketful of Hope
Gordon Parks

I photographed poverty in many parts of the world. The worst I saw in Brazil where I found Flavio. He was a 12-year-old boy slowly dying of asthma, tuberculosis and malnutrition. 1

Flavio lived in the favella, a sweating slum of rich, elegant Rio de Janeiro, and home to him was a hillside jumble of squatters' huts that sat beneath the statue of Christ that looms over the 2 city. Despite his misery and illness, Flavio cared for his six brothers and sisters while his mother and father worked for, at the most, $25 a month. Each day was filled with fighting and tears, hunger and dirt. Flavio cooked what little there was to cook and attacked the one room each morning with a broom and what little water he could spare—water he carried on his head a mile up the slippery hill. Humanity had all but forgotten him, yet he was so strangely human. I constantly wondered how that frail body got the strength to love when love seemed to have been so absolutely denied to it. He always managed a little painful smile when I approached, as if I had brought along a pocketful of magic hope.

"Mamma says only the lucky ones die young in favella," he   3 told me one day. And times without number, I saw the fathers impassively carrying the yet-unembalmed lucky ones down the slopes. In Flavio's favella, tears were for those who die old, for it was they who knew the misfortune of long life on this hill of human waste and sorrow.

QUESTIONS

1. What techniques of writing in "No Pocketful of Hope" indicate that Gordon Parks is a reporter with a camera? Relate a zoom lens to the movement of the description.
2. Point out differences in the author's treatment of background and of Flavio.
3. What is the purpose of the description? What is the advantage of the I-was-there approach?

WORD STUDY

(1) dying of . . . *malnutrition*, (2) he was so *strangely human*, (3) the fathers *impassively* carrying, (4) the *yet-unembalmed* lucky ones, (5) this hill of *human waste*.

The Flip-Flop Machines
John Kobler

A large-scale computer assembly soothes the eye and ear. In   1
an immaculate room, air-conditioned to protect the delicate
circuitry against the heat of the electrical current coursing
through it, the floor raised on braces to accommodate cables
underneath, stands a phalanx of sleek boxes, spray-painted in
pastel shades of gray, red, blue, yellow. Glass panels permit a
partial view of their insides—minute colored lights winking
like myriad fireflies, silvery reels of tape spinning. Invisible
below, wiring by the mile, relays, switches and transistors emit
a gentle hum. From softly click-clacking teleprinters, as they
record the computer's statements, sheaves of paper rustle to the
floor. The attendant staff engineers, technicians and program-
mers move with the hushed, furrow-browed absorption of peti-
tioners at an oracle.

As I began to learn something about high-speed electronic   2
digital computers, I was astonished by the contrast between the
complexity of the problems they solve and the simpleminded
way they go about it. It is a truism that they do arithmetic like
an ordinary desk calculator, only faster. Still more astonishing,
a computer knows only one kind of arithmetic. It knows how to
add. But that is all it needs to know in order to perform every
possible arithmetical computation, since subtraction is simply
the addition of a minus number, division is repeated subtraction, and multiplication is repeated addition. To multiply, for
example, 937,846,229 by 738, the computer adds the first figure
to itself 738 times.

The anatomy of a computer has five main organs. Their re-   3
spective functions are crudely analogous in the human system
to vision, memory, analysis, brain and communication. Its vision,
an input mechanism, receives the description of its task, along
with pertinent data and step-by-step instructions on how to
manipulate the data. This material may come from punch cards,
magnetic tape, disks, a teletypewriter. It originates with the
programmer, the human "software," who converts numbers and
letters into computer code. With photoelectric cells, metal

From THE FLIP-FLOP MACHINES by John Kobler. *The Saturday Evening Post,*
May 4, 1968. Reprinted by permission of the author.

brushes or other feelers, depending on the medium, the computer senses the presence or absence of punched holes, magnetic spots, etc., and converts them into electric pulses.

Its memory, an aggregate of tiny magnetized ferrite rings, 4 stores this input until the successive arithmetical steps call for it. The analysis unit, where the actual computation goes on, encloses a network of circuits, which transform the pulses received into new patterns of pulses, representing the additions. The brain, the central processor, containing another maze of circuits, controls the entire operation, directing traffic to and from the memory, guiding pulses into the appropriate channels, and ordering the sequence of steps. Within split seconds the organ of communication, an output mechanism, delivers the result, converted back into numbers and letters.

QUESTIONS

1. In Paragraph 1, what are the key words of the topic sentence? Underline descriptive details relating to color and sound.
2. What contrast is presented in Paragraph 2? How does the contrast help describe computers?
3. In Paragraphs 3 and 4, what analogy is developed? How does this analogy help readers visualize computers?
4. Make a brief outline showing the organization of the description. As you list main points and subheadings, keep this central idea in mind: A computer soothes the eye and ear, works like a simple-minded mathematician, and has functions similar to those of the human brain.

WORD STUDY

(1) to protect the delicate *circuitry*, (2) a *phalanx* of sleek boxes, (3) like *myriad* fireflies, (4) an *input* mechanism, (5) an *aggregate* of tiny magnetized *ferrite* rings.

Outward Bound at Night

Brooks Atkinson

Amid the glitter and vitality of an autumn evening in New 1
York, the departure of the ship is melancholy. All the radiance
originates and is contained in New York.

Lying alongside Pier 3 in the North River, the ship holds 2
her head toward a cheerful wall of lights on West Street, where
civilians are totting up the day's accounts. Everything associated with the city looks lively. The bright lights on harbor tow-
boats seem to race up and down the river. The Staten Island
ferry, ablaze with lights, looks like a royal barge as she sweeps
up the bay in the center of a moving pool of shining water.

When the light at the end of Pier 3 turns from red to green, 3
the S. S. *Esparta* blows a warning signal and slowly backs into
the stream, where the rushing tide cants her stern downriver.
Every maneuver the ship makes is deliberate, as if she were an
intruder. A railroad tug and a barge slide by with the dash and
heedlessness of an enterprise that owns the city.

After the ship has lumbered around, she moves cautiously 4
toward the channel. Everything she leaves behind looks bright,
eager and confident. The Statue of Liberty with her thin golden
crown holds the torch of freedom high in the sky and gives the
bay her timeless blessing. Manhattan Island with its forest of
slender buildings is a pyramid of light. Since the contours of
the buildings have disappeared into darkness, the island looks
as if it had no material substance. It is the peak of a community
of light that encloses the dark bay in shining ribbons. Above the
city the sky is filled with a glow that looks festive.

But the channel is solitary and joyless. When the ship passes 5
the buoys on the starboard side, they give doleful hoots, for
they are part of an intricate network of warning that controls
the movement of ships. The network says "no," in contrast with
the city that says "yes." As the ship enters the Narrows she
passes under the center of the Verrazano Bridge, which looks
tall from the shore but dangerously low when the foremast
glides under the cables. Passing under this lofty bridge gives
the alarming illusion of being a near thing.

Now the ship is leaving the girdle of lights and is headed for 6 blackness of night at sea. Since the water is livelier outside the bay, the starboard buoys hoot more anxiously; and on the port-side the buoys with bells give dismal clangs when the wash tips them from side to side. They sound like a witches' chorus.

In the blackness at the foot of the channel the Ambrose   7 Lightship cuts the night with sharp glares in a tireless series of flashes. Since wind is now pouring off the ocean, it is cold on deck. All the warmth seems to have been left behind with the hospitable incandescence of the city. "Rig the ladder on the portside," someone on the bridge bellows. The ship begins to lose way; and the pilot cutter, looking alert and competent, swings around the ship's stern and softly nudges the port quar-ter. After scrambling down the ship's ladder, the pilot steps to the dancing deck of the cutter, where a deckhand steadies him. Then the cutter is off with a putter of diesel engines.

The ship picks up speed. In the freezing darkness of the   8 lonely night she heads for Barnegat Light and then settles on a southern course (course 181) for the island of Jamaica, 1,445 miles away.

QUESTIONS

1. Upon what basis does Brooks Atkinson arrange his descriptive details?
2. How would deletion of the personal reactions, judgments, or moods of the author affect the description?
3. Point out specific allusions that heighten the realism of the word picture.
4. Which descriptive details best highlight the contrasts?
5. How does the conclusion relate to the introduction?

WORD STUDY

(1) the ship has *lumbered* around, (2) gives the bay her *timeless* bless-ing, (3) a *pyramid* of light, (4) *doleful* hoots, (5) the *hospitable incan-descence* of the city.

Robert Doisneau, RAPHO GUILLUMETTE PICTURES

SUGGESTIONS FOR WRITING

1. Write a description similar to the description from "No Pocketful of Hope." Stress your observations rather than your opinions or your actions. Be in the picture, but do not dominate it. Zoom in on what you see, as Gordon Parks does.

   Suggestions:
   a. passenger on a bus
   b. a football player on a bench
   c. a suspect in a line-up

2. After reviewing "The Flip-Flop Machines," write a composition describing a thing or a place. Whether you describe ocean liners or a laundromat, Xerox machines or an assembly plant, try to present a clear word picture that makes your reader see what you see, sense what you sense. Keep in mind the importance of size, color, shape, and motion.

3. Use "Outward Bound at Night" as a model for a descriptive composition. Present effective contrasts, such as silence and noise, darkness and light, coldness and warmth.

   Suggested topics:
   a. landing at an international airport
   b. the ending of a football game (*or* an exciting movie)
   c. a launching at Cape Kennedy

4. Use the photograph on page 173 as the basis for a descriptive composition on life in an apartment house. To make your reader see or imagine, be generous with descriptive details.

Organizing factual materials

One type of expository writing is the presentation of organized factual materials. You collect numerous facts on a particular subject and then decide upon a "handle" or central idea. This idea, the nucleus of your organization, ought to indicate the interrelationship as well as the significance of your factual materials. Or you may decide upon the central idea and then use it as a basis for your selection and organization of facts. Either way, your purpose in writing this type of composition is to share carefully organized information.

Don't Look Back
George D. Hendricks

A multitude of motifs in proverbs, folk sayings, folk beliefs, and folktales warn us against looking back. Some few tell us that we *should* look back. As expressions of the folk, these ideas involve basic psychological problems and indicate serious and usually valid philosophical outlooks upon life. 1

There are, of course, two ways to look back: one is in a physical or directional sense, involving space; the other is chronological, involving time. In both of these senses there are dangers to be avoided and values to be sought; these dangers and values may be internal or external. 2

DON'T LOOK BACK by George D. Hendricks. From *Singers and Storytellers*, edited by Mody C. Boatright, Wilson M. Hudson, and Allen Maxwell. Southern Methodist University Press, 1961. Reprinted by permission of the Texas Folklore Society.

Don't cry over spilled milk. Wipe the slate clean and start 3
from scratch. Bury the hatchet. Let sleeping dogs lie. Let bygones be bygones. Don't give it a second thought. That's water
under the bridge. Burn your bridges behind you. Such are the
sayings everybody knows. Whoever follows the dictates of these
sayings believes that somehow things will turn out all right in
spite of what has gone before. He is, in this sense, essentially
a man of faith.

Even nursery rhymes imply the same disregard for troubles 4
of the past or present, the same confidence in the future:

> Little Bo Peep has lost her sheep
> And can't tell where to find them.
> Leave them alone and they'll come home
> Wagging their tails behind them.

> Mary had a little lamb.
> Its fleece was white as snow.
> And everywhere that Mary went,
> The lamb was sure to go.

Neither Bo Peep nor Mary need worry about what's behind
them. If their animals are well trained, they will follow.

Some folk cures prohibit the backward look. For removing 5
warts, take a penny you have earned from your mother. Give
it to her and ask her to rub it three times with her thumb. Then
take it to the back door and turn around and throw it over your
shoulder into the back yard. If you don't look back at it, and if
you never try to find it, your warts will go away. If you have no
faith in this cure, it simply won't work.

Other superstitions practiced the world over, from ancient 6
times to the present, also demand that a person have faith. If
you see a load of hay, make a wish and look away (without confidence you cannot have your wish). If you put on underwear
wrong side out, you must leave it that way. If you discover you
have left something important at home, you must not go back
after it. To do so is to bring on bad luck. If you decide to take
the risk anyway, you must sit down, take a deep breath, say
"damn it," take your hat off, turn it around three times, spit
over your left shoulder, and replace your hat. It is doubtful,
however, that this will remove your apprehension.

Both folk and literary proverbs warn us against looking back. 7
Remorse is the echo of a lost virtue, according to one American

proverb. Plutarch wrote, "Memory is to us the hearing of deaf actions, and the seeing of the blind." Longfellow wrote that we should let the dead Past bury its dead. Sandburg writes, "The Past is a bucket of ashes." And Shakespeare wrote, "What's past is prologue."

Certainly a man's attitude is conditioned by his emphasis upon a segment of time—whether it be past, present, or future. 8

QUESTIONS

1. How does George D. Hendricks relate the items of his folklore collection?
2. What do the nine sayings in Paragraph 3 have to do with the values mentioned in Paragraph 2? Can you discern the principle of selection of materials in Paragraph 3? Why do you suppose the author did not include Longfellow's "There are no birds in last year's nest"?
3. In Paragraph 4, how are the examples of nursery rhymes related to a "man of faith," mentioned in Paragraph 3?
4. How are the folk cures listed in Paragraph 5 related to the title and to preceding paragraphs? What do the superstitions in Paragraph 6 have to do with the central idea of the article? In Paragraph 7, what do all of the proverbs have in common?
5. If you deleted all of the examples (and references to them) in "Don't Look Back," how much of the essay would remain? How many sentences?

WORD STUDY

(1) A multitude of *motifs* in proverbs, (2) these dangers and values may be *internal* or *external*, (3) the *dictates* of these sayings, (4) your *apprehension*, (5) *folk* and *literary* proverbs.

The Pressures Generated by Abundance

Vance Packard

It may seem odd that affluence should undermine privacy, but it clearly has. There is evidence that much of the great increase in surveillance, investigation, and intrusion into people's privacy can be traced to conditions arising from abundance. 1

Consider the problem of launching and moving goods in today's superabundant economy. Styles in products are changing swiftly. The lifetime of product *types* is becoming ever shorter. And, there is increasing strain to find significantly new products or variants. All these factors have produced a greater preoccupation with secrecy. A company concerned with secrecy in industry begins to wonder who can be trusted and brings in the undercover agents to check on employees. 2

This pressure to move goods affects individual privacy in another way. Companies have been turning to more relentless selling tactics to attract our attention. Privacy diminishes as the hawkers telephone us several times a week, or shove their feet in the door while posing as survey markers. 3

Affluence has produced a tremendous increase in the use of credit and in the sale of all sorts of insurance policies. The sellers of both credit and insurance feel that to survive they must investigate the lives of prospects. Every insurance policy, for example, is a risk, a bet. The companies try to hedge their bets on policies of substance by arranging for a quiet investigation of the insured's finances and living habits. And so we have millions of insurance investigations, often accompanied by a "neighborhood check"—and the findings often reach files from which information is swapped or sold. 4

The growth in the amount of spare time that most Americans can enjoy has in at least one way made privacy more difficult to achieve for many of them. Americans have more time now to read newspapers, magazines, and books and to watch TV and listen to radio. They want not only to be informed but to be entertained and, often, titillated. Many enjoy gossip and scandalous 5 facts about fellow citizens. And many of the mass media have relentlessly sought to provide them with a steady diet of gossipy information. The result of both the desire for such information and the media's efforts to supply it has in effect produced a combined assault on privacy. The dual nature of this assault is pointed up by Morris Ernst and Alan Schwartz in their definitive legal analysis of privacy as it is affected by the media.* At one point they note that the desire "of the mass media to make a profit at the expense of our privacy is a growing pressure." And they ask: "How should the ever-increasing thirst of the public for news and information be balanced against the sometimes desperate desire for privacy on the part of the individual?"

Finally we might simply note sociologist Kingsley Davis' 6 observation that the explosive growth of both possessions and people "is causing an ever larger portion of our high level of living to be used to escape from the consequences of congestion."

QUESTIONS

1. What is Vance Packard's central idea, his nucleus of organization?
2. What evidence does the author use to support his central idea?
3. What do Packard's selected facts about insurance companies indicate?
4. What do leisure time and the mass media have to do with our "naked society" or our lack of privacy? How are these related to the title of the article?
5. How does Packard conclude? Why do you suppose he did not decide to end with a summary?

WORD STUDY

(1) the great increase in *surveillance*, (2) a greater *preoccupation* with secrecy, (3) to more *relentless* selling tactics, (4) as the *hawkers* telephone us, (5) to be entertained and, often, *titillated*.

---

* Morris L. Ernst and Alan U. Schwartz, *Privacy: The Right to Be Let Alone,* Milestones of Law Series (New York: The Macmillan Company, 1962).

Tornadoes: Forecasts and Warnings

Bernard Vonnegut

The threat from tornadoes has diminished somewhat, thanks   1
to several developments. After a destructive twister hit Tinker
Air Force Base, near Oklahoma City, two Air Weather Service
officers, E. J. Fawbush and R. C. Miller, began analyzing data
from many such events. They finally perceived a special, rather
complicated set of circumstances that included an intruding
"tongue" of warm, moist air in the lower part of the atmosphere,
dry air above it, and at a higher altitude a strong wind called the
jet stream. This combination often creates the extraordinarily
severe thunderstorm that breeds a twister. The new prediction
idea isn't infallible, but it has worked most of the time and was
an enormous step forward. Before long the U.S. Weather Bureau,
following this exciting lead, was routinely forecasting the probability of tornadoes.

Another important advance uses radar for early warning   2
and to pinpoint the tornado's location. Besides giving a maplike
picture showing storm activity over a radius of several hundred
miles, it indicates the height of clouds in the storm system.
Tornadoes seldom come from ordinary thunderstorms—those
less than eight miles high. The probability increases, radar op-
erators have learned, when the clouds build to ten or twelve
miles, penetrating well into the stratosphere. In addition, radar
may show what is perhaps an indicator of the tornado itself—a
small hooklike echo on the edge of the storm system. This clue
can indicate the tornado's probable course.

Another warning method came from what almost everybody   3
who listens to an ordinary AM radio set knows—thunderstorms
bring static. Each lightning flash behaves like a powerful trans-
mitter. In ordinary thunderstorms each discharge of lightning
produces bursts of noise, at a rate of only about 10 per minute.
But from tornado producers the electrical noise is almost con-
tinuous, easily imagined to sound like gravel pouring onto a
sheetmetal roof. People in tornado country have used such static
as a warning of trouble.

The radio noise has been studied by Herbert L. Jones,   4

Professor of Electrical Engineering at Oklahoma State University. Sensitive radio direction-finding equipment has shown that the bursts average over 1,000 per minute, easily distinguishing the tornado-producer from ordinary thunderstorms. In many cases the bearing of the maximum noise informs Jones where the tornado is located in the radar echo of its mother storm.

Also helpful is modern society's network of high-speed communications. The new tornado is usually spotted promptly by amateur or professional weather observers, often also by state police or civil defense networks. Broadcasters can then interrupt their programs with warnings to people in threatened areas. This may not do much to reduce property damage, but today's forecasts and warnings certainly give people time to take proper precautions, thereby greatly reducing the annual toll of deaths and injuries.   5

QUESTIONS

1. In Paragraph 1, what facts does Bernard Vonnegut use to show that it is now possible to forecast probable tornadoes?
2. In Paragraph 2, what facts tell how radar is used for pinpointing a tornado?
3. According to Paragraphs 3 and 4, what does radio noise reveal about tornadoes? What does a tornado-producing storm sound like on the radio?
4. Why do you think the author placed the facts in Paragraph 5 last? Why not first?
5. What transitional devices are used to link the paragraphs of the article?

WORD STUDY

(1) The new prediction idea isn't *infallible,* (2) penetrating well into the *stratosphere.*

SUGGESTIONS FOR WRITING

1. Find a motif from folklore comparable to "Don't Look Back." Organize a composition based on that motif. Secure interest by drawing examples from familiar materials. Or perhaps you would prefer to choose a motif from popular songs, stories, or jokes.

Wallace Kirkland, RAPHO GULLUMETTE PICTURES

2. Vance Packard's article deals with the pressures of affluence on privacy. List examples of your own as evidence that the pressures of affluence affect much more than privacy. Find a central idea to fit your examples, and base a composition on that idea.

3. Write a composition presenting organized factual materials. Use "Tornadoes: Forecasts and Warnings" as a model.
   Suggested central ideas:
   a. Modern advances in medicine are making us immortal.
   b. Everybody today can cook—with a little water and a lot of instant products.
   c. Because of recent inventions, bugging is no longer an art.

4. Americans are bombarded daily with "facts" about their health; they are advised to take this medicine or that, to quit smoking, to get rid of fat, to jog or swim, to try yoga, and so on. In a carefully organized composition, present your own selected facts that you believe every health-conscious American should know.
   Suggested title: Maintaining Good Health.

Classifying information

To classify is to put into groups, to pigeonhole. For instance, you might classify college dropouts according to credits earned before leaving (freshmen, sophomores, juniors, seniors) or according to academic potential (the genius, the plodder, the deficient) or according to interests (husband-hunters, the sports-minded, identity-seeking rebels) or according to other systems of division—on the basis of sex, religion, politics, financial status.

As you read the following selections, notice that when a writer classifies information he first states his method of classification or his point of departure. He then goes quickly to a discussion of each class. The usual procedure is to devote one or more explanatory paragraphs to identifying, defining, describing, illustrating, or evaluating each class.

Modern Poverty
John Kenneth Galbraith

One can think of modern poverty as falling into two broad   1
categories. First there is what may be called *case* poverty. This
one encounters in every community, rural or urban, however
prosperous that community or the times. Case poverty is the
poor farm family with the junk-filled yard and the dirty children
playing in the bare dirt. Or it is the grey-black hovel beside the
railroad tracks. Or it is the basement dwelling in the alley.

Case poverty is commonly and properly related to some characteristic of the individuals so afflicted. Nearly everyone else has mastered his environment; this proves that it is not intractable. But some quality peculiar to the individual or family involved—mental deficiency, bad health, inability to adapt to the discipline of modern economic life, excessive procreation, alcohol, insufficient education, or perhaps a combination of several of these handicaps—have kept these individuals from participating in the general well-being.

Second, there is what may be called *insular* poverty—that which manifests itself as an "island" of poverty. In the island everyone or nearly everyone is poor. Here, evidently, it is not so easy to explain matters by individual inadequacy. We may mark individuals down as intrinsically deficient; it is not proper or even wise so to characterize an entire community. For some reason the people of the island have been frustrated by their environment.

This is not the place to explore in detail the causes of insular poverty. They are complex and many of the commonly assigned causes are either excessively simple or wrong. The resource endowment or the fertility of the land, the commonplace explanations, have little to do with it. Connecticut, a state of high incomes, has few resources and a remarkably stony soil. West Virginia is richly endowed. Connecticut has long been rich and West Virginia poor.

Insular poverty has something to do with the desire of a comparatively large number of people to spend their lives at or near the place of their birth. This homing instinct causes them to bar the solution, always open as an individual remedy in a country without barriers to emigration, to escape the island of poverty in which they were born. And so long as they remain they are committed to a pattern of agricultural land use or of mining, industrial, or other employment which is unproductive, episodic, or otherwise unremunerative. Meanwhile the poverty of the community insures that educational opportunities will be limited, that health services will be poor, and that subsequent generations will be ill prepared either for mastering the environment into which they are born or for migration to areas of higher income outside. It is a reasonable presumption, too, that the homing instinct operates most powerfully among the poorly educated.

In some circumstances escape may not be possible. Especially in the urban slum, race or poverty may confine individuals to an area of intrinsically limited opportunity. And once again the environment perpetuates its handicaps through poor schools, evil neighborhood influences, and bad preparation for life.

QUESTIONS

1. What is the central idea of "Modern Poverty"?
2. According to Galbraith, how many types of modern poverty are there? How is each type explained?
3. Where is case poverty found? What are the characteristics of persons afflicted by it?
4. Where is insular poverty found? What does the "homing instinct" have to do with it? When is escape not possible?
5. Why do you suppose Galbraith devotes more space to insular poverty than to case poverty?

WORD STUDY

(1) it is not *intractable*, (2) excessive *procreation*, (3) *intrinsically* deficient, (4) without barriers to *emigration*, (5) employment which is unproductive, *episodic*, or otherwise *unremunerative*, (6) a reasonable *presumption*, (7) the environment *perpetuates* its handicaps.

A New and Different Generation
Paul Woodring

When old-timers undertake to assess the faults and virtues of   1
the young they are likely to take one of three basic positions. The
most venerable is that the younger generation is going to the
dogs, a view that was popular with the Greeks and Romans and
has appeared in the literature of nearly every period since classi-
cal times. Pundits throughout the ages have proclaimed that the
youth of their day were lazy, immoral, irresponsible, and dis-
honest. They have predicted that these young people would

From A NEW AND DIFFERENT GENERATION by Paul Woodring. From *The Higher Learning in America* by Paul Woodring. Copyright © 1968. Used with permission of McGraw-Hill Book Company.

never be able to accept adult responsibilities and that consequently civilization would decline. And they have not always been mistaken. Greek culture did fall into ruin; the Roman Empire, after a period of moral dissolution, declined and fell apart.

It is possible that the twilight of Western civilization is upon 2 us, as Spengler predicted, but a half century after his *Decline of the West* appeared his predictions still seem premature. There is indeed much disorder and conflict within our culture as well as a notable loss of confidence in the future, but there is also still a great deal of rugged vitality. Though in some members of the younger generation, as well as in some of our own generation, there is evidence of a loss of nerve and of the kinds of moral degeneration that accompanied the fall of Rome, there is as yet no clear evidence of a collapse in the culture as a whole. If the culture eventually does disintegrate, there will be no logical reason for blaming the younger generation, or the older generation, for the collapse. The causes will go deeper and farther back.

A second view, frequently expressed by optimistic com- 3 mencement speakers, is that his is the best of all possible generations—that today's students are more virtuous, better motivated, and more enlightened than any that have gone before; and that as a result we can face the future with confidence that a better world lies just ahead. This view is too blandly optimistic for my taste; it ignores too many symptoms of profound illness within the society, including some segments of the younger group. There is no very good reason to believe that this younger generation, when it moves into positions of responsibility, will be able to solve the world's problems much better than we have done.

A third view, popular with elderly professors of the Mr. 4 Chips variety, is that one generation is very much like another. Young people must always go through a period of adolescent rebellion during which they find it difficult to accept the rules and regulations that govern adult society; each generation thinks itself the first to have discovered sex and liquor, but this is all just a matter of growing up. According to this view the present generation, a few years after graduation, will become very much like its parents—moderately virtuous, moderately industrious, moderately law-abiding, and moderately stuffy. All it will take is a little time, a job, a marriage certificate, three or four children, and a house bought on the installment plan.

There is, of course, an element of truth in this. Many ado- 5 lescent rebels do become conservative adults, not because of age but as a result of new responsibilities and a growing vested interest in the *status quo* that makes rebellion seem less desirable. But this view fails to take into consideration the fact that each generation is a product of its own times and develops its special character in response to the pressures, challenges, and opportunities it faces. If today's youth are substantially different from those of earlier days, as I think they are, it is because they have grown to maturity in a different world.

QUESTIONS

1. Does the first sentence state the central idea of the whole article or of only the first paragraph or of both?
2. What three classifications of attitudes does Paul Woodring select? Are these three views currently widespread?
3. If you were the author of this composition, would you add a fourth category? Would the belief that "young people don't know the value of a dollar" parallel the other classifications of Woodring, or would this notion fit within one of his three views?
4. Which paragraphs state and explain the three classifications? What techniques of paragraph development are used for each?
5. What is the controlling idea of Paragraph 2? of Paragraph 5?

WORD STUDY

(1) *Pundits* throughout the ages, (2) a period of moral *dissolution*, (3) moral *degeneration*, (4) too *blandly* optimistic, (5) elderly professors of the *Mr. Chips* variety.

SUGGESTIONS FOR WRITING

1. Taking the approach of "Modern Poverty," write a composition that classifies information.
   Suggested subjects:
   a. modern pageantry
   b. TV epidemics
   c. current slang
   d. habitual discontent
2. Put into practice some of the writing techniques of Paul Woodring as you write a composition classifying information.
   Suggested titles:
   a. Youth Sizes Up Age
   b. Slobs Understand Snobs (or vice versa)
   c. Employees Read the Minds of Employers

3. Classify information in a composition based on one of the following central ideas. A few possible categories are in parentheses.
   a. New-breed theologians are changing American Churches. (Methodists, Baptists)
   b. We have many dreams in common. (of falling, of flying)
   c. There are three kinds of eyebrow lifters. (the bridge or poker player, the dean of women or men)
   d. College students enjoy various types of music. (electronic, impressionistic, vocal, folk, instrumental)

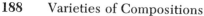
Bill Cote

Explaining a process

When you write a composition to explain a process, you may discuss what habitually happens or what has already taken place. For example, you may explain the stages in the growth of an embryo or trace the origin and development of the jury system. Or you may show what could happen as you explain a procedure for getting desired results. For instance, you may give step-by-step instructions for making a poster from a slide or for transplanting prickly cactus.

A process involves change. Since change involves time, you may decide to arrange your materials chronologically. You will probably find useful such transitional words as *first, second, next, after, then, when, later, immediately, as, while, soon, in the meantime, in a few minutes, within a week's time, finally.*

As you read the next four selections, notice the kinds of processes explained. Observe the transitional words as well as the method of organization.

FROM
Hawaii
James A. Michener

For eons of time the two massive volcano systems stood in   1
the sea in fiery competition, and then, inevitably, the first began
to die back, its fires extinguished, while the second continued to

pour millions of tons of lava down its own steep flanks. Hissing, exploding, crackling, the rocks fell into the sea in boundless accumulations, building the later volcano ever more solidly, ever more thickly at its base on the remote floor of the ocean.

In time, sinking lava from the second master builder began to creep across the feet of the first, and then to climb its sides and finally to throw itself across the exposed lava flows that had constituted the earlier island. Now the void in the sea that had separated the two was filled, and they became one. Locked in fiery arms, joined by intertwining ejaculations of molten rock, the two volcanoes stood in matrimony, their union a single fruitful and growing island.

Its soil was later made from dozens of smaller volcanoes that erupted for a few hundred thousand years, then passed into death and silence. One exploded in dazzling glory and left a crater looking like a punch bowl. Another, at the very edge of the island, from where it could control the sea approaches, left as its memory a gaunt headland shaped like a diamond.

QUESTIONS

1. What is the controlling idea of James A. Michener's three paragraphs?
2. Point out transitional words relating to time.
3. Can you discover the author's principle of paragraph division? Why are there three paragraphs instead of one?
4. What is it about Michener's style that makes his writing different from an encyclopedic entry giving essentially the same information?

WORD STUDY

(1) *eons* of time, (2) the second *master builder*, (3) the *void* in the sea, (4) *intertwining ejaculations* of molten rock, (5) a *gaunt* headland.

How To Prune Roses

The Editors of Southern Living

Roses need pruning to control the size of the plants, to remove dead wood and diseased growth, and to encourage strong, healthy growth capable of producing an abundance of blooms. 1

Pruning roses is not as difficult a task as avoiding pricks from their thorns while you're pruning. Before you start trimming, remember there's an ideal time and a correct way to prune roses. Soon after the last killing frost is the ideal time. You should start with sharp, sterilized shears. Rubbing alcohol will clean them satisfactorily. 2

In removing dead, weak, and diseased-looking wood, cut back to the base of the growth—to the ground or back to a healthy cane. Leave no stubs. Cut away any branches that interfere with the plant's good form, and remove any twiggy growth. Remove any leaves that have persisted over winter—they may harbor diseases. Cut out all weak canes or branches that are growing inward toward the center of the bush. 3

In pruning for new growth and blooms, leave three to five strong canes. Cut tea roses back to a height of 12 to 18 inches. With floribundas, it is often advisable to leave more canes of longer length (24 to 30 inches), depending on their location in the landscape. On the strong canes you are leaving, be sure to make each cut at a 45-degree angle just above a single, well-developed growth bud. Begin cut $\frac{1}{4}$ to $\frac{1}{2}$ inch above the bud, starting the cut at a point on the cane opposite the bud. 4

After pruning, coat the end of each cut with tree paint or pruning compound to keep out borers. Use a small paintbrush or a liquid shoe polish applicator. Some pruning compounds are marketed in pressurized spray cans. 5

QUESTIONS

1. What is the purpose of Paragraph 1?
2. Point out the paragraphs that tell the reader what to do (a) before, (b) during, and (c) after pruning his roses.

HOW TO PRUNE ROSES by the Editors of *Southern Living*, February 1970. Reprinted by permission of *Southern Living*.

3. What contributes to the clarity of the procedure described in Paragraphs 3, 4, and 5? How do the diction and sentence structure differ from Michener's in the selection from *Hawaii?*

WORD STUDY

How much does word choice contribute to the clarity and the simplicity of the directions? What is the difference between leaves (a) *that persist over winter* and those *that are left over after winter,* (b) *that harbor diseases* and those *that have diseases?*

Appendix A: How to Take Notes
"Brevity and Conciseness Is the Soul of Note-taking,"
Leander Gormley, '02

From the Yale Record

THE PROFESSOR SAYS:	YOU WRITE DOWN:	
"Probably the greatest quality of the poetry of John Milton, who was born in 1608, is the combination of beauty and power. Few have excelled him in the use of English language, or for that matter, in lucidity of verse form, *Paradise Lost* being said to be the greatest single poem ever written."	"Milton—born 1608."	1
"When Lafayette first came to this country, he discovered America, and Americans, needed his help if its cause were to survive, and this he promptly supplied them."	"Lafayette discovered America."	2
"Current historians have come to doubt the complete advantageousness of some of Roosevelt's policies."	"Most of the troubles and problems that now face the United States are directly traceable to the bunglings and greed of President Roosevelt."	3

APPENDIX A: HOW TO TAKE NOTES, from the *Yale Record.* Reprinted with the permission of Yale University.

"... it is possible that we do not completely understand the Russian viewpoint."	"Professor Mitchell is a Communist."	4
"Pages 7 through 15 are not required but will prove of unestimable worth to the student in preparation for the term examination."	"Omit pages 7 through 15."	5
"Socrates was a Stoic, but it should be pointed out that Stoicism is very different than cynicism. A cynic is contemptuous of all things, especially human nature, whereas a Stoic is one who accepts all things as they are without complaining."	"Socrates was a cynic."	6
"The examination will test the student's over-all comprehension of the subject, and a thorough knowledge of theories behind the facts and their relevance to fields other than Political Science will be absolutely necessary."	"Bull exam."	7
"... the papers will be marked on a scale ..."	"Bull exam."	8
"The class Friday will probably be the most important of the year since we will throw it open to a general discussion of the main problems which have come to our attention throughout the course. Attendance will not be taken."	"No class Friday."	9
"George Washington, incidentally, loved apple pie and there is an unimportant but amusing story in this connection. One day he was walking down the street with a book in his hand and happened to meet a young lady who was carrying a bunch of apples, and ..."	"George Washington loved unimportant but amusing stories. One day he was walking down the street looking for a piece of apple pie when he met a girl with a bunch of books in her hand and ..."	10

"We come now to the well-known theory of relativity. The student must remember that time, motion, and many such connected concepts are not absolute but actually relative, or referred to another concept. Thus when we walk past a tree, we are not *really* walking past a tree, but actually the tree is partially walking past us, since . . ."

"Write Jane Monday 11 night."

QUESTIONS

1. How does the subtitle give focus to "Appendix A: How to Take Notes"?
2. Are any of the notes as stated sensible or practical?
3. How does this selection on how to take notes differ from "How To Prune Roses"? (Point out differences in form, organization, word choice, sentence structure, mood, and purpose.)

WORD STUDY

(1) *lucidity* of verse form, (2) *Stoic*, (3) *cynic*.

How a Pond Freezes and Thaws

David Webster

Most people who live in northern climates have witnessed   1
the icing up of a pond. The events leading to the freeze-up—
which occurs suddenly in a day or two—take place gradually
over a period of several months. These events are important to
the aquatic life that must spend its winter sealed under the ice.
By late summer the pond reaches its maximum water temperature, and then, as the days shorten and the chill of autumn ar-
rives, the pond begins to cool. When this happens the water at
the top of the pond cools first, contracts, and becomes heavier.

HOW A POND FREEZES AND THAWS, from "An Improbable Solid" by David Webster. *Natural History*, March 1968. Reprinted by permission of *Natural History*.

The heavy water sinks to the bottom, pushing warmer, lighter water to the top. This natural circulation is known as "pond turnover." Some of the oxygen on which aquatic animals depend during the winter comes from air that is dissolved in the water as it circulates; so, the longer pond turnover continues, the greater the winter oxygen supply will be. Pond turnover continues until the water reaches a uniform temperature of 39°; then as the water expands, turnover halts.

2 In the first stages of freezing, the pond becomes edged with a paper-thin ring of ice. Even though the air temperature may be colder than that of the soil and rocks, water is cooled much more quickly by contact with denser materials. Soon the entire surface of the pond is covered with a layer of thin clear ice. This gradually thickens and appears black, because it allows one to view the dark water below through the ice layer.

3 As long as the weather remains cold, the thickness of ice increases, but at a diminishing rate. If the air temperature reaches 10° during the night, the temperature of the ice gradually becomes equally as cold, causing more water to freeze along its undersurface. As the air warms up during the day, the ice acquires a uniform temperature of 32°. Soon the thick ice so effectively insulates the unfrozen water from the cold air above that very little additional ice is formed.

4 After a few weeks black ice usually becomes white ice. The milky color is caused by gas bubbles that are trapped underneath. This trapped gas is a by-product of decay and photosynthesis, because as long as the icy surface of the pond remains free of snow, sunlight and heat can pass through it. Thus, the normal life of the pond continues, sealed away from winter temperatures. If, however, the pond becomes covered with snow, sunlight is blocked and photosynthesis stops. If this situation continues for any length of time, winterkill occurs, usually destroying most of the life in the pond. Larger bodies of water take much longer to freeze completely. Deeper water remains free of ice long after shallow ponds have frozen over.

5 The thawing of ice takes place as rapidly as does its formation, often accompanied by loud cracking and booming, depending on the size of the body of water. Much of the melting occurs on the undersurface of the ice, since the heat of the sun is conducted through the ice to the pond water and heats it a few degrees above the freezing point. Even if the air above the ice is many degrees warmer this is still the case. The same principle holds for an ice cube; in water it melts much more rapidly than in air at the same temperature or even warmer, because heat is conducted to the ice more rapidly by water than by air. Initially,

the ice disappears from the places where it formed first. Large cracks appear and the entire surface begins to break up. Within a week's time the pond is again ice free. Perhaps this event was best described by Henry David Thoreau: "I looked out the window, and lo! where yesterday was cold gray ice there lay the transparent pond already calm and full of hope as in a summer evening, reflecting a summer evening sky in its bosom, though none was visible overhead, as if it had intelligence with some remote horizon."

QUESTIONS

1. Why is David Webster's choice of the process of the freezing and thawing of a pond more interesting than, say, the process of aerobic respiration?
2. Does David Webster arrange his materials chronologically? How much time does the process of freezing take? How long is the process of thawing?
3. Relate the facts in Paragraphs 3 and 4 to those in Paragraph 2.
4. Is paragraph 5 climactic? Why or why not? How does the quotation from Thoreau contribute to the unity of the selection?

WORD STUDY

(1) pond *turnover*, (2) a by-product of decay and *photosynthesis*, (3) *winterkill* occurs, (4) some *remote* horizon.

SUGGESTIONS FOR WRITING

1. Write a composition explaining a process: like James A. Michener, you may discuss what has already taken place; or like David Webster, you may explain what usually happens.
   Suggested topics:
   a. the birth and development of one of my best ideas
   b. the gradual dissolution of a high-school friendship
   c. how storm clouds form, build, and dissipate
2. Write a composition explaining a step-by-step procedure for getting desired results. You may decide to be serious and use as your model "How to Prune Roses." Or, like the author of "Appendix A: How to Take Notes," you may prefer to be facetious or ironic.

Bruce Roberts, RAPHO GUILLUMETTE PICTURES

Suggested topics:
    a. how to fry chicken
    b. how to defend yourself
    c. how to study for finals
    d. how to treat a common cold
    e. how to cast a horoscope

3. Look at the photograph of the hands as it is printed above. Then turn the picture on its side, and turn it upside down. Write a composition based on the differences in effect that you noticed as you turned the photograph. The composition could be entitled "How to Communicate."

Supporting an argument

Argument deals with controversial issues. As you argue, you may act like a fighter or like a referee. As a fighter, you debate and advocate action that will knock out opposition and gain the approval of the crowd. For example, you may argue for or against mercy killing and urge others to support or reject such killing, to accept your views and act on them. As a referee, you survey a controversial arena, announce your decision, and hope that others will understand and accept your position. For instance, you may decide whether or not marriage and funeral ceremonies should be abolished and present your views persuasively, while realizing that your argument will not instigate action or change the world. Whether you write as a fighter or a referee, a crusader or a judge, you should always include reasons why you believe as you do.

Unless the title itself is a question, before each argument that follows is an italicized controversial question that may be answered with a *yes* or a *no*. As you read each article, give special attention to the way each author presents his answer, the way he supports his side of the controversy.

Malcolm X: Demagogue or Martyr?

C. Eric Lincoln

As soon as Malcolm was dead his critics turned on him with 1
the fervor of self-righteousness and his defenders sought to
elevate him to sainthood and martyrdom. On the one hand, it
was pointedly suggested that as a demagogue and a spokesman
for violence Malcolm somehow deserved what he got at the
Audubon ballroom that Sunday, the day before Washington's
Birthday. He had been a thug, an addict, and a thief, it was
argued; he was an ex-convict;. he had made no contributions
whatever to society.

There is a *non sequitur* here which honesty compels us to 2
examine. It is contrary to the "American ideal" and Christian
morality to hold a man's past against him if it can be shown that
he has overcome that past. Man *is* redeemable; if he is not, surely
preaching is in vain. Malcolm X rose above the errors of his
youth. Whether or not one agrees with his solution to the race
problem, it must be admitted that during the years he presumed
himself a race leader he was, under the constant scrutiny of a
hostile public, far more circumspect than many of our more
"respectable" leaders and politicians. If anything, his past
seemed to give him a unique insight into the nature of the problems with which he sought to deal. We owe it to him and to ourselves to acknowledge the facts.

On the other hand, those who saw in the returned pilgrim to 3
Mecca a "new" Malcolm X were at best probably premature in
their judgments. The underlying cause of the breach between
Malcolm X and Elijah Muhammad was not so much a contest of
power within the movement as a conflict of ideology. Malcolm X
was a true revolutionary. It is not inconceivable that, given the
time, the means, and the opportunity, Malcolm X would have
committed an act of violence.

He was indoctrinated to believe that racial strife is the in- 4
evitable means of bringing about a reversal of the black man's
status, and he passionately believed in and longed for that reversal. True, his conversion to Islam and his desire to be ac-

ceptable to orthodoxy may have ameliorated his aggressive tendencies; but the evidence that at the time of his death he was prepared to join the nonviolent crusade is scanty, if indeed it exists at all.

Malcolm X must be taken for what he was. He was a remark- ably gifted and charismatic leader whose hatred and resentments symbolized the dreadful stamp of the black ghetto, but a man whose philosophies of racial determination and whose commitments to violence made him unacceptable as a serious participant in peaceful social change. He had ideological followers —far more than the handful of men and women who belonged to the Organization of Afro-American Unity. His spirit will rise again, phoenix-like—not so much because he is worthy to be remembered as because the perpetuation of the ghetto which spawned him will not let us forget.

QUESTIONS

1. What is the purpose of the introductory paragraph?
2. What does *non sequitur* mean? How is this term related to argument?
3. How does C. Eric Lincoln's argument differ from that of (a) self-righteous critics and (b) sainthood seekers?
4. According to the last three paragraphs, was Malcolm X a demagogue or a saint? What does the author believe Malcolm X was really like (a) as a convert to Islam and (b) as a revolutionary? What does Malcolm X now symbolize to the author?

WORD STUDY

(1) may have *ameliorated* his *aggressive* tendencies, (2) gifted and *charismatic* leader, (3) *ideological* followers, (4) His spirit will rise again, *phoenix-like*.

Needed: Tolerance and Participation

The Editors of Time

The students have taught the university administration two
lessons: 1) some of the changes that they want are really im-
provements, and 2) the way to deal with student power is to
anticipate it, to initiate changes before the students demand
them. Administrators who have permitted students to participate
in some policy areas applaud the results, say that it prevents
protest and often raises standards. Students should be permitted
to voice their opinions on dormitory rules, on the performance
of professors, and on what courses should be added or dropped.

But there is an all-important difference between student advice and student control. If students could dictate the hiring and
firing of professors, they would tend to select those with whom
they agree—and fall into an echo chamber. Latin American
students have considerable control over many universities, and
the consequence is chaos and inferior education. A university
is not a democracy and cannot become one without degenerating
into anarchy. At a conference on "Students and Society" at Cal-
ifornia's Center for the Study of Democratic Institutions last
year, the president of the student body of St. Louis' Washington
University put it aptly: "Were Washington University to be
turned over to the students and faculty, it would fold in about six
months because nobody would know how to run it."

Both the students and the elders have some other lessons to
be learned. What is needed most of all is more mutual respect.
The student activists are more critical than constructive. They
often have no immediate, practical answers for the problems that
they expose—but older people should not lightly dismiss them
for that. Sometimes it is enough just to ask the right questions.
Student protests have stirred authorities in Spain, Germany and
other countries to some fitful steps toward modernization. And
students have begun to move U.S. universities in some desirable

directions—toward a more involved role in the local community, toward a rethinking of the relevance of education.

For their part, the students might recognize that they do not   4
have a monopoly on idealism. After all, the drives against poverty and racism in the U.S. were energized not by them but by their elders. It would also profit the students to recognize the temporary nature of their power and the severe limits on it. Theirs is primarily the power to disrupt. They can interfere with the established authority, but they cannot change it without help from other powerful groups in the population—as Czech students learned in their successful protest and Polish students learned in their unsuccessful one. With that in mind, activist students might do more to court allies not only among their more moderate contemporaries but also among older people. In this, they are not helped at all by some of the retrogressive tendencies of the extremists: they are often intolerant of anyone who disagrees with them, all too willing to interfere with the rights of others, and sometimes ready to stoop to hoodlumism and fascist methods.

Student power can be beneficial; student tyranny never is.   5
Student involvement in politics should be encouraged, but student abuse of the democratic process must always be resisted. Students might well bear in mind the fine distinctions between reasoned dissent and raw intolerance, between knowledge and wisdom, between compromise and copping out. Students have much more to gain by working actively for change within the existing system than by dropping out of it.

QUESTIONS

1. List in order the main points of the argument in "Needed: Tolerance and Participation."
2. According to the editors of *Time*, what have administrators learned from students? Why are some administrators supporting students who have protested?
3. What examples are given of student advice? of student control? When do the editors believe that student power stops being beneficial and starts becoming tyrannical? How are students intolerant? How can they become wiser?
4. What actions are recommended for administrators? for students?
5. Using your dictionary as a starting point, decide what the "fine distinctions" are "between reasoned dissent and raw intolerance, between knowledge and wisdom, between compromise and copping out."

(1) fall into an *echo chamber*, (2) without *degenerating* into *anarchy*, (3) more *mutual* respect, (4) a *rethinking* of the *relevance* of education, (5) a *monopoly on idealism*, (6) the *retrogressive* tendencies of the *extremists*, (7) ready to *stoop* to *hoodlumism* and *fascist methods*.

Should the home be a democracy?

A Bill of Rights for Children

Joshua Loth Liebman

Throughout the ages religion has created an enormous Bill 1
of Rights for parents. Now has come the time when we have to write a Bill of Rights for children as well. In the home at its best we should have a system of checks and balances, a democracy that avoids the extreme on the one hand of tyranny, where the father plays the role of dictator—or the mother stars in the drama as the omnipotent ruler—or on the other hand an extreme of anarchy in which there are no laws, no rules, no accepted code of behavior or discipline. Sons and daughters cannot develop their fullest potentialities in either a despotism or an anarchy. They will emerge from the walls of the family sanctuary twisted and distorted in some fashion or other if they have been compelled to submit to the decrees of a father or a mother tyrant, or, on the other hand, if they have received from the parental atmosphere no firmness, no justifiable frustration, but only overindulgence or overprotection that ill prepares them for the genuine realities of the world of men and of women.

The goals as I see them, then, are the establishment of a de- 2
mocracy in the home, and in this little republic of the family, parents must recognize that their sons and daughters are personalities in their own right, not mere pawns on a chessboard of parental ambition or vanity. What a great liberation will come to the world when fathers and mothers realize that they do not own their children merely by virtue of the biological accident of

birth, and when they come to see that the little infant or the growing boy or the adolescent daughter possesses the inalienable rights given to every human soul by God, and not merely the specific rights bestowed by the omniscient and all-powerful parent. The tragedy which is too little recognized in our age is that in this acquisitive society some fathers and mothers make their children their possessions; if they do not possess enough stocks or bonds or material things in the world of prestige, they often attempt to make their offspring their compensation for failure or disappointment in the great race of life, and look to their sons and daughters to compensate them for all the blocks and obstacles in their quest for ego-satisfaction.

If a home is to be a democracy, the children have to be respected as personalities in their own right and a climate has to be fashioned for them—a climate of consistency and of predictability. What do I mean by this? I mean that there should be a dependable emotional atmosphere in which the child is raised. It should be a temperate zone. A child cannot stand a parental environment which is 98 degrees in the shade of love one hour and 20 degrees below zero of rejection the next hour. Make no mistake about it: boys and girls seek discipline as well as devotion, firmness as well as love; but the firmness should be well defined and mutually understood and should not be merely the expression of an angry mood or an irrational caprice. Predictability and probability are now great words in science, for without them no mastery of physical nature is possible. Well, boys and girls depend on predictability in the attitudes of their parents, just as much as the chemist depends on other natural laws in his laboratory. I do not mean to suggest that fathers and mothers should go around taking their own and their children's emotional temperatures all the time. Occasional outbursts of parental anger or fits of moodiness are both normal, and are relatively unimportant so long as the boys and girls have been given an unwavering sense of emotional security and know with all their hearts that they are loved, wanted and respected. A certain stability on the part of parents is obligatory, a consistency which will make possible the beginning of a democracy in the home.

QUESTIONS

1. What is the controlling idea of Joshua Loth Liebman's argument?
2. According to Liebman, what present evils stem from the fact that children have no Bill of Rights?

3. Exactly how will a children's Bill of Rights eradicate these evils?
4. What does the author mean by a "climate of consistency and of predictability" in a democratic home?

WORD STUDY

(1) an *enormous* Bill of Rights for parents, (2) the mother stars . . . as the *omnipotent* ruler, (3) their fullest *potentialities*, (4) the walls of the *family sanctuary*, (5) *justifiable frustration*, (6) on a *chessboard* of *parental ambition* or *vanity*, (7) the *inalienable* rights, (8) the *omniscient* and all-powerful parent, (9) this *acquisitive* society, (10) their *quest* for *ego-satisfaction*.

Is Communism monolithic?

Communism Is Not a Monolithic Monster

Thomas A. Bailey

Ever since the Bolshevik Revolution in Russia, countless worried peoples in the free world have assumed that Communism was one gigantic and granitic monolith, and that Communist parties all over the globe took their orders from Moscow like soldierly robots.   1

Communism, though presenting a fearsome front, has never been monolithic. Lenin and Trotsky were never in complete agreement as to the course their world revolution should take, and after Lenin died and Stalin came into power, Trotsky was exiled and later murdered. A tiny following of Trotskyites still lingers in the United States and elsewhere.   2

In 1948 the defection of Marshal Tito of Yugoslavia advertized to the whole world the rift within the Communist fold. In the years since then we have also witnessed the noisy rupture between Moscow and Peking. Elsewhere throughout the Communist world we have noted the stiffening resistance to dictation or even guidance from Moscow, and we have even observed the   3 cut-throat rivalry between the Red Soviets and the Red Chinese for control of the emerging nations, especially in Africa.

On the one hand, the furious quarreling within the Communist camp is to the advantage of the free world, for it weakens the might of our most potent adversary. On the other hand, it promotes fanatical irresponsibility, as in the case of Red China. The age-old game of divide and conquer may be working to the advantage of the United States, provided that we play our cards right.

The more countries that go Communist, the less monolithic Communism becomes and the more infighting develops. The policymakers in Washington have evidently not given this profound truth the emphasis it deserves. If we had permitted Vietnam to go Communist after the Geneva Agreements (disagreements) of 1954, a united Vietnam, if its previous history meant anything, might have resisted Chinese control. If so, the free world might have benefited from a species of Far Eastern Titoism.

In brief, the more Communism spreads, the more Titoism there is bound to be, and this, though risky, is a relatively inexpensive way of fighting Communist attempts to revolutionize the world. If the Reds cannot agree among themselves how to dominate the globe, they are less likely to dominate it.

Even the presumably formidable Communist parties in countries like France and Italy are less alarming than their sheer numbers portend. Most of their members are evidently first of all nationalists, without any desire to submit to foreign dictation. More often than not they join the Communist party as a means of protesting against existing parties or of supporting local reforms.

QUESTIONS

1. What impact does the choice of words have on the presentation of the viewpoint in Paragraph 1? Why do you think Thomas A. Bailey chose "gigantic and granitic monolith" instead of "a tyrannical form of government"? Why "soldierly robots" instead of "docile or obedient citizens"?
2. Is the first sentence of Paragraph 2 the central idea of the paragraph or of the entire argument?
3. How does the author use facts about (a) the murder of Trotsky, (b) cut-throat rivalry, and (c) the spread of Communist domination to *support* his argument?
4. What persuasive techniques are used? How convincing are they?

(1) *Monolithic* Monster, (2) the *defection* of Marshal Tito, (3) the *rift* within the Communist *fold,* (4) our most *potent adversary,* (5) the *presumably formidable* Communist parties.

Are the basic principles of existential politics right?

Existential Politics

Arthur Schlesinger, Jr.

Not only do men who claim infallibility in politics do far   1
more evil than good, but the systematic suppression of sup-
posedly false ideas would deeply impoverish human knowledge
and understanding. "There is no error so crooked," Tupper said,
"but it hath in it some lines of truth." Or, as Norman Mailer re-
cently put it, "Sometimes a profound idea is buried in a particularly ugly notion." Human creativity takes a marvelous and
sinister diversity of forms. How dare anyone assume the right to
deny the unlimited freedom of human expression? "I tolerate
with the utmost latitude the right of others to differ from me in
opinion without imputing to them criminality," wrote Jefferson.
"I know too well the weakness and uncertainty of human reason
to wonder at its different result."

The demand for the forcible suppression of "false" ideas   2
would be an enormously effective way of calling a halt to human
progress. And the other half of the new creed makes no more
sense: that is, the conviction that one should feel and act first
and think later, that the struggle generates the blueprint and the
means create the end. The kind of action supremely required
to strike through the mask of official society, we are told, is
violence. Without violence, official society, in its present sophis-
tication, will calmly co-opt and emasculate the opposition. Only
violence will force official society to drop the smiling mask of
tolerance and reveal its inner viciousness. More than this, vio-

lence becomes a means of social and individual redemption. As Franz Fanon has written, "Violence is a cleaning force. It frees the native from his inferiority complex and from his despair and inaction; it makes him fearless and restores his self-respect. . . . Violence alone, violence committed by the people, violence organized and educated by its leaders, makes it possible for the masses to understand social truths."

This is hardly, of course, a novel doctrine. Others in this 3 century have eloquently propagated the cult of the deed. It was, after all, Mussolini who used to distinguish between "a violence that liberates, and a violence that enslaves . . . a violence that is moral and a violence that is immoral." And it was Hitler who wrote, "The very first essential for success is a perpetually constant and regular employment of violence." It is perfectly obvious why Mussolini and Hitler favored violence: because violence, by abolishing the procedures and civilities of society, opens the way for those who are most adept in the mobilization of force. I do not know about the situation in developing countries; there violence in certain contexts may have the beneficial effects claimed by Fanon. But surely little is more pathetic than the view that in American society violence will benefit the left. A limited amount of collective violence may stimulate the process of democratic change; but, if the left, through the cult of the deed, helps create an atmosphere which destroys the process of democracy itself, the only winners will be those who use violence best, and they will be on the right.

The new creed, with its dismissal of free discussion and its 4 conviction that violence will mystically generate policy and program, represents an assault on rationality in politics—an assault based on the ultimate proposition that rights and wrongs in public affairs are so absolute and so easily ascertainable that opposition can be legitimately destroyed. This assault on the Bill of Rights and on libertarian democracy is in my judgment wrong, because no one is infallible. It is stupid, because the beneficiaries will not be the idealists of the left but the brutalists of the right. It is dangerous because it represents a reversion to and rationalization of the strain of hatred and violence in our own national tradition: the politics of lynch law against the politics of Lincoln. The New Left, in this respect, casts its vote for the worst against the best in our political ethos.

Above all, the new creed overlooks the fact of human frailty. 5 "Men are not flattered," wrote Lincoln, "by being shown that there has been a difference of purpose between the Almighty and them." Yet men are not gods. That is why absolutism always fails in human society. Democracy requires consent—it insists, that is, that a majority of the electorate eventually be persuaded that one course is preferable to another. If men or mechanisms were infallible, there would be no need for such persuasion. But, because they are not, the discipline of consent is indispensable to civilized society. The discipline of consent means that policies must triumph not through the divine right of kings or of a "democratic educational dictatorship" but through making sense to a majority of the people; and the condition of bringing a majority along is the best guarantee that policies relate, not to private fantasy or personal power, but to the greatest good of the greatest number.

Nietzsche once wrote, "Gaze not too deeply into the abyss, 6 lest the abyss gaze into you." Those who claim to *know*—to be the bearers of absolute truth—are men who have gazed too deeply into the abyss. They have committed what Hawthorne called the Unpardonable Sin—the sin of self-pride, which enslaves people, breeds fanaticism and concludes in madness and catastrophe. It is sad when the derelicts of our society surrender to the Unpardonable Sin; it is contemptible when our intellectuals exemplify it. Let us strike out against the concrete evils of our time. But let us not yield to that awful despair which dissolves all distinctions in thought and action and hurtles us on to the politics of apocalypse. In the long run, any sane society must rest on freedom and reason. If we abandon this, we abandon everything.

QUESTIONS

1. What basic principle of existential politics does Arthur Schlesinger, Jr., refute in Paragraph 1? How are selected quotations from Tupper, Mailer, and Jefferson linked?

2. What is the purpose of the first sentence of Paragraph 2? What is the controlling idea of Paragraph 2? Notice the four dots indicating an omission in the quotation from Franz Fanan. Give possible reasons why the author chose not to quote every word of the passage.

3. What does the first word of Paragraph 3 refer to? Why does the author single out Hitler and Mussolini for discussion?

4. In Paragraphs 4 and 5, what reasons does Schlesinger give to support his argument?

5. Consider both the content and the style of the final paragraph as you evaluate the conclusion of the argument.

WORD STUDY

(1) *co-opt* and *emasculate* the opposition, (2) eloquently *propagated the cult* of the deed, (3) an *assault on rationality* in politics, (4) *libertarian* democracy, (5) a *reversion to* and *rationalization of* the strain of hatred, (6) *absolutism* always fails, (7) the *discipline of consent* is *indispensable.*

SUGGESTIONS FOR WRITING

1. Using "Malcolm X: Demagogue or Martyr?" as your model, write a composition presenting an argument based upon your strong opinions of someone whose reputation is controversial. Begin with a summary statement of opposing views, especially those that clash with your own. Show how these views are rash judgments or half truths as you present and defend your position.
2. Write a composition using the title "Needed: Tolerance and Participation." Use the essay on page 202 as your model, but shift the subject from campus disruptions to religious or political controversies. Or, if you disagree with the editors of *Time,* write a rebuttal, assaulting their ideas, point by point. Support your argument with specific, convincing reasons.
3. Answer a controversial question with a resounding *yes* or *no.* Then base a well-organized argument upon your answer. You should refer to "A Bill of Rights for Children" for a model.
   Suggested controversial questions:
   a. Should the high school be a democracy?
   b. Should all college courses be electives?
   c. Should mercy killing (*or* bigamy) be legalized?
   d. Should college athletes receive large scholarships?
4. Review Thomas A. Bailey's method of argument in "Communism Is Not a Monolithic Monster." Then take an unusual point of view as you write a composition supporting an argument to alleviate the fears of those who disagree with you. Use many specific facts closely connected with those fears, facts that tend to spawn the fears, to *support* your argument.
   Suggested titles:
   a. UFO Inhabitants Are Not Little Green Martians
   b. The Next War Will Not Be Universal Suicide
   c. Male Supremacy Is Not a Myth
5. Write a composition of indignation, hotly arguing against two or three basic principles of a creed that you detest. Model your composition after Arthur Schlesinger's "Existential Politics." Use

strong diction, persuasive facts, relevant quotations. End your
argument with an appeal, a challenge, or a threat.

6. Is God dead? Is it only man's notion of God that lives? Does
organized religion govern the relationship between God and
man? Write an argument giving your views about the place of
religion in the seventies.

Formulating a definition

When you devote a whole composition to a definition, your purpose is to provide your reader with more information than a college dictionary affords. You may begin by explaining the need for a clear definition of a word or idea and then proceed by formulating that definition—giving the word's category, pointing out its limits, and differentiating it from similar terms. You may discuss its etymology as well as its connotations and provide numerous examples to illustrate your meaning. Notice how the authors of the next two essays formulate definitions.

Junk
George R. Stewart

Like most of the related terms, *junk* is vague in meaning. 1
It is like the non-putrescible fraction of garbage, except that it consists of material too bulky or objects too large to be squeezed into the can. Size, not kind, is of the essence. A small transistor radio goes out as garbage; a large set goes as junk. From that point the size ranges upward to old cars and trucks, and eventually to old locomotives, airplanes, and steamships. So also, paper bags and wrappers, along with scattered newspapers, go into the can, but waste paper in bulk and newspapers in bundles are an important element in junk. Just as junk cannot altogether

JUNK, from *Not So Rich As You Think* by George R. Stewart. Houghton Mifflin Company, 1968. Reprinted by permission of Houghton Mifflin Company.

be distinguished from garbage, so also it is only differentiated from *trash* and *rubbish* in a vague manner. As opposed to these two, junk implies a possible re-use.

Thus conceived, junk is the basis of many thriving businesses. There is even an association of such businesses, but in the interest, or imagined interest, of public relations, the junk-dealers are organized as the National Association of Secondary Material Industries. The subdivisions of this association indicate the chief materials of their commerce, that is, the Paper Stock Institute, the Textile Division, the Scrap Rubber and Plastic Institute, and three institutes or divisions dividing among themselves the enormous commerce in metal scrap.

Junk, both as a conception and as a term, has little history behind it. The word itself, traditionally existing only in the English language, may be traced from the fifteenth century, when it meant an old and worn rope. A seaman's term, it was probably derived from the Portuguese, in their century of notable achievement in seafaring. *Junca* means a reed in Portuguese, and of reeds a kind of cheap and inferior rope was made. Such ropes did not wear long, and so the derogatory suggestion of the word easily developed. Once worn out, these ropes were cut up to serve for oakum or boat-fenders, and *junk* thus began to assume its modern suggestion of "secondary material." By the eighteenth century, British and American seamen were applying the word in a general derogatory sense, as when salt-beef was called junk. It was also used for miscellaneous collections of worn, secondhand, and cheap goods. Shops which stocked such materials for the outfitting of seamen came to be called junk shops. Only toward the end of the nineteenth century, however, first in the United States and later in Great Britain, did the word begin to assume its modern meaning— used material, of a certain bulk and durability, chiefly conceived by the consumer as something to be got rid of, but salvable under favorable circumstances.

Junk, therefore, is something new and characteristic of our own time. The future archaeologist will reconstruct this civilization from the rich harvest of junk heaps. The present archaeologist, studying the past, has no such chance. The chief material of which he can make use is the plentiful supply of broken pots. Even these, we can suppose, were often mended instead of being thrown away. A thoroughly broken pot, however, was apparently beyond salvage, even in the poverty-stricken days of the early historical period. First the Industrial Revolution and then the Age of Affluence have combined to produce junk.

QUESTIONS

1. How do *The American Heritage Dictionary* and the *Oxford English Dictionary* define *junk?* List ways that George R. Stewart either deviates from or supplements the dictionary definitions.
2. Why do you think the author defines *junk?* Why devote a whole paragraph to the history of the word? Why is the focus on junk rather than on trash or garbage?
3. What distinction is made between junk and garbage? What examples are given?

WORD STUDY

(1) *vague* in meaning, (2) the *non-putrescible* fraction of garbage, (3) the *derogatory* suggestion of the word, (4) *salvable* under favorable circumstances, (5) apparently beyond *salvage*.

What Is a Bachelor?
Corey Ford

What is a bachelor? Well, as I see the typical unmarried male—and I see him in the mirror every morning while shaving —he is somewhere in his fifties, a little on the paunchy side, and inclined to be bald. Usually he wears a sweater and an old pair of corduroy pants, with a blanket around his legs to protect him from drafts. (He's very sensitive to drafts.) His address book, if he could find it, is filled with the names and dates of his god-children's birthdays. The only female who visits his apartment regularly—it isn't a penthouse, by the way—is the cleaning woman, and she is Polish and several times a grandmother. He turns in as a rule at ten, because there's no reason to stay up, and rises again at six, because there's no reason to stay in bed.

It was the late H. L. Mencken who defined a bachelor as a man whom no particular woman ever decided to marry. I hesitate to differ with such an eminent authority on the sexes (though it is only fair to point out that Mencken was married), but I feel

1

2

this definition falls a little short of the whole story. Bachelor-ship is more than being single; it is a philosophy, a way of life, and singleness is only a part of it. Not every unmarried man is a bachelor. Ours is a very exclusive fraternity, with strict entrance requirements, and the lack of a wife is not enough in itself to qualify a candidate for membership.

We don't take in hermits, for example. A man who leads a 3 solitary existence is never exposed to women, and consequently has no experience at eluding them. He is like a rabbit which has never faced the hounds. He lacks the speed of foot, the instinct for proper evasive action when cornered at a social soirée, the knack of dodging into a thicket of guests or losing the trail around the buffet table, the skill of doubling back on his conversational tracks to throw a pursuer off the scent, the ability to wriggle out of a trap, which marks the successful bachelor. The first female hunter to invade his lonely lair would nail him point-blank with one shot.

Likewise our admissions committee frowns on the unmar- 4 ried man with a mistress. The *chère amie* whom he maintains is apt to be far more attentive than most wives, fetching his slippers and lighting his pipe and stroking his forehead when he is sad. Save for a few legal technicalities, he is in fact a husband. I'll grant that such an arrangement is subject to change without notice, but, after all, so is marriage. His Jezebel is devoted to him and he in turn is dependent on her, and will quit his bachelor friends in the midst of a poker game and hurry home to be with his beloved doxy. His attendance at the club falls off, until the other members demand his resignation.

Anyone who has ever had a wife, needless to say, is black- 5 balled automatically. Once a man starts marrying, it's hard to stop. A divorced husband may swear up and down that he's learned his lesson and is cured for life; but let some titian-haired temptress plop onto his knee and run her fingers over his bald spot, and a week or so later his friends will receive a post card from Acapulco, where he's spending his honeymoon. By the same token, a widower is taboo. Even if he fails to marry again, the memory of his late-lamented will always linger in his mind, and in the midst of a quartet at the bar he'll suddenly break down and start telling everyone, in a choked voice, that she was the swees lil wminaworl. Obviously you can't have that sort of thing going on around a bachelor club.

Nor do we admit a man who has stayed single for purely 6 economic reasons. The parsimonious male who refuses to take a wife because of the expense involved is considered unworthy of the high standards of our fraternity. Similarly we exclude neurotic types with mother complexes, men who do not wed because it would interfere with their careers, or—most deplored of all—misanthropes who hate the whole female sex. Your true bachelor doesn't object to women. All he objects to is marrying them.

QUESTIONS

1. Why do you think Corey Ford defines a bachelor? Which word choices help achieve his purpose? What are the advantages of the I-was-there approach?
2. How is the "typical unmarried male" or bachelor limited or restricted in regard to (a) his physical appearance, (b) his association with females, and (c) his reasons for staying single?
3. How does the bachelor differ from other unmarried males, such as hermits, divorced husbands, widowers, men with mistresses?

WORD STUDY

(1) a little on the *paunchy* side, (2) at a social *soirée*, (3) *chère amie*, (4) His *Jezebel*, (5) his beloved *doxy*, (6) *titian-haired* temptress, (7) she was the *swees lil wminaworl*, (8) The *parsimonious* male, (9) *neurotic* types, (10) *misanthropes*.

SUGGESTIONS FOR WRITING

1. Using "Junk" as a model, write a serious composition formulating a definition of a word. Begin with a statement of purpose. Use comparisons and examples. Be sure to make distinctions between the word you are defining and other words similar to it. Use the *Oxford English Dictionary* for pertinent facts regarding its history. End by stressing its relevance as currently used.
   Suggested words:
   a. pastry
   b. red tape
   c. integration
   d. claustrophobia
2. Write a light composition similar to "What Is a Bachelor?" Follow the usual pattern of a formal definition, as does Corey Ford. But use informal diction and make absurd distinctions to amuse or entertain your reader.

Suggestions:
- a. a bachelor girl
- b. a sophomore
- c. a matchmaker
- d. a Jezebel

3. Can an emotion be defined? If you think so, use the photograph below as the inspiration for a composition defining an emotion like loneliness, grief, wonder, love, or any other emotion this photograph may suggest to you.

Michael Keller

Making an analysis

An analysis is a close examination of the parts of a whole. When you make an analysis, you take something apart for study and then present a statement of your findings or an opinion based upon the results of your study.

Suppose, for example, that you have chosen the subject of handwriting. When defining, you could simply explain what handwriting is, distinguish it from printing, and give examples; when classifying, you could discuss various types of handwriting, ranging from hen scratches to a scrawled flourish; when analyzing, you could first look at individual strokes or letters and then present your conclusions about the meaning of what you have observed.

Footprints
Immanuel Velikovsky

In numerous places and in various formations are found   1
footprints of animals of prehistoric times. Those of dinosaurs and other animals are clearly impressed in rock. The accepted explanation is that these animals walked on muddy ground, and their imprints were preserved as the ground became hard and stony.

This explanation cannot stand up against critical examina-   2
tion. On muddy ground one may find impressions of the hoofs

of cattle or horses. But the very next rain will smudge these impressions, and after a short while they will be there no more.

If we do not find the hoofprints of cattle that passed along a path the season before, how is it that the toe imprints of animals of prediluvial times remain intact in the mud on which they walked?

The imprints must have been made like impressions in soft sealing wax that hardens before they are blurred or obliterated. The ground must have been soft when the animal ran upon it, and then it quickly hardened before changes could take place. Sometimes we see imprints of animals that chanced to walk over freshly laid concrete. While the substance was soft, a dog or a bird or a large insect might have walked on it and left impressions recognizable when it hardened. Also, heated sand, turning into a viscous substance on its way to becoming hardened glass, could receive and preserve imprints. The vestiges could also remain in muddy, unheated ground that was soon covered by lava which filled in the imprints and later disintegrated on being weathered away. In historical times—in the volcanic destruction of Pompeii and Herculaneum—lava and volcanic ashes filled the wheel tracks in the streets of these cities and thus preserved them to our day. In the eruption of Kilauea in Hawaii in 1790, when many people lost their lives, and with them a brigade of the Hawaiian army, the footprints of trapped humans and animals were retained in the hardened volcanic ash.

Wherever footprints in the ground dating from historical or prehistoric times are found, we may assume that most probably a catastrophe took place when these vestiges were left or very shortly thereafter. If a catastrophe was in progress or was threatening, the animals must have been in terror and flight. The footprints actually show that the animals in most cases were fleeing, not wading or loitering about; sometimes the configuration of the impressions indicates that an animal was indecisive, probably trapped by some peril closing in from all sides.

The animals that were in flight for their lives may have succumbed a few moments later, crushed or burned in the disaster. The ground was swept by driven sand and ashes or covered by lava or asphalt, or cement, or fluid silicon, then possibly covered by floods, and the imprints in the heated soil that was baked to stone have survived to the present day. So it is that we do not find tracks of animals that peacefully walked one hundred or three hundred years ago, but we do find traces and vestiges of animals that walked and ran many thousands of years ago.

QUESTIONS

1. What is the accepted explanation for the footprints that Velikovsky is discussing?
2. As Velikovsky considers how impressions harden, how does he relate footprints to sealing wax, to concrete, to heated sand, to lava and volcanic ash?
3. After his close examination, why does Velikovsky refute the accepted explanation?

WORD STUDY

(1) animals of *prediluvial* times, (2) they are *blurred* or *obliterated*, (3) turning into a *viscous* substance, (4) and later *disintegrated* on being weathered away, (5) traces and *vestiges* of animals.

Your Language Says More Than You Think
Mario Pei

Some years ago on the radio a popular show was conducted 1
by Professor Henry Lee Smith, now of the University of Buffalo. He would undertake, usually with remarkable success, to identify what regions the program's guests came from by asking them to pronounce certain words to which regional custom has given noticeable twists. He seldom made a mistake, and when he did, it was due to what he called a mixed pattern (a person born and brought up in one locality, then transplanted to another place where he would, after years of residence, give up some of his original speech features and take on those of his adopted home). This he accomplished by using a series of imaginary east-west and north-south lines, which form the boundaries between one form of expression and another. His reasoning went something like this:

YOUR LANGUAGE SAYS MORE THAN YOU THINK by Mario Pei. From *The Many Hues of English*, Random House, 1967. Reprinted by permission of Charles C. Thomas, Publisher, *Police* Magazine. Relevant portions reprinted from *Think* Magazine, published by IBM, Copyright © 1958 by International Business Machines Corporation.

This man pronounces *merry, Mary,* and *marry* in three different fashions; this places him east of the Alleghenies. He says *greasy,* not *greazy;* this puts him somewhere north of a line running between Trenton and Philadelphia. His use of *wahsh* instead of *wush* and his use of *dawg* for *dog* and *lahg* for *log* confirm this (*dawg* and *lawg* identify a second area, *dahg* and *lahg* a third). He uses the same *a* in *park* that he uses for *father,* and that eliminates most of New England, as does his use of the same flat *a* for *ash* and *ask.* He uses the same vowel in *horse* and *hoarse,* which means that he comes from the area between Philadelphia and New York. But his *first* sounds a little like *foist,* and this eliminates Philadelphia. So I would place him within a radius of no more than thirty miles from Times Square.

After listening to other speakers, Dr. Smith, all ears, would confidently state that they were from the Tidewater section of Virginia, or the vicinity of Pittsburgh, or southwestern Indiana. Occasionally he would come out with a statement like: "You sound like a man born in eastern Texas who has lived for more than ten years in or near Washington, D.C." And he would generally be right.

There was no magic about Dr. Smith's performance—only long, hard work put in on the *Linguistic Atlas of the United States* and many, many native speakers, resulting finally in a series of valid generalizations.

The man born and bred east of the Alleghenies, whether north or south, generally avoids pronouncing his final *-r,* while the Midwesterner and Westerner usually pronounce it very distinctly and audibly, sometimes almost painfully so. The same goes for an *r* before a consonant inside a word (*father* and *farther,* for instance, will sound pretty much like *fahthuh* in eastern speech). The Easterner will give the same pronunciation to *horse* and *hoarse, for* and *four,* while the Westerner will use for *hoarse* and *four* the vowel sound of *so. Wush* or *wursh* for *wash, darter* for *daughter, paw* and *maw* for *pa* and *ma,* belong to the Midwest. The Southerner will tend to say *aig* for *egg, fin'* for *find, kep'* for *kept, chile* for *child.* The New Englander outside the Boston area will *park* his *car* with the *a* of *bat* and no audible *r,* but the Bostonese will use in *ask* and *bath* practically the same *a* he uses in *father.* A large part of the Ohio Valley will say what amounts to *beyit* for *beat,* and even *giyit* for *get.* The typical New Yorker may or may not say *boid* for *bird* and *erl* for *oil,* but unless he is educated out of it he will replace the *th* of *three* with *t,* and the *th* of *this* with *d.* He will pronounce *wetting* and *wedding* the same way and use *bo'uhl* for *bottle.* He will use the same *ng* in *singer* that he uses in *finger,* and if the

2

3

4

5

ng comes at the end of a word and the next word starts with a vowel, he will carry the *g* over (*gettin gout* for *getting out*). The *ou* of *about the house* will sound peculiar in the mouth of either a Virginian or a Canadian, but the Virginian will surround it with Southern features and drop his final *-r*, the Canadian will talk like a Midwesterner and pronounce his *-r*.

Not only in the way they pronounce words but also in their choice and combination of words, people reveal their origins. What an Easterner calls a paper "bag" a Midwesterner would call a paper "sack," and a Southerner might easily call a paper "poke." What many people call a Coke might be a "tonic" in parts of New England, a "soft drink" in many parts of the nation, a "dope" in parts of the South. Anyone who calls a green pepper a "mango" is almost certainly from the Midwest, most probably from Ohio. If a large sandwich is called a "hoagy," a "hero," or a "poorboy," it would be a clue that the speaker is respectively from Philadelphia, New York, or the South. "You bet" used for "You're welcome" or "Don't mention it" identifies a speaker generally as a Midwesterner, particularly from the Chicago area. Philadelphians say "square" and "pavement" for what others call "city block" and "sidewalk." Where most people "park" cars, residents of Trenton "rank" them, and those of southern Delaware "file" them.   6

These differences, while purely local, are still fairly legit-   7
imate English. Beyond them are out-and-out dialects and slang usages that take liberties with the English language. "Get shut of" for get rid of and "jin" for do hard work are characteristic of the Ohio Valley. "Cabbage onto" for get hold of would identify a native of Oklahoma, and "I don't belong to get up till nine a.m.," a native of Idaho. Southern girls are sometimes "carried," rather than taken, to dances. The Pennsylvania Dutch have contributed such speech mannerisms as "the milk is all [gone]," "outen [put out] the light," and "the paper wants [predicts] rain." If the speaker uses "youse" in addressing a plural audience, he is likely to be from the New York area; if he says "you-all," he is more likely to be from the South; "you-uns," and even an occasional "us-uns" for we marks him as coming from the mountain region of the Appalachian divide.

QUESTIONS

1. How does Mario Pei secure reader interest in Paragraph 1?
2. What sentence in Paragraph 2 unifies the specific facts?

3. How are various dialects analyzed? What, for example, are some of the linguistic differences between an Easterner and a Westerner?
4. If Mario Pei had omitted all the supporting details, what main ideas would be left? How convincing are these bare statements without the supporting evidence?

WORD STUDY

(1) in a series of *valid generalizations*, (2) the *Bostonese* will use, (3) *out-and-out dialects*.

SUGGESTIONS FOR WRITING

1. Pretend that you have come from another country and entered your first English class; everything there is completely foreign to you. Look around and find a subject to analyze—a human being, a plastered wall, a window, a pencil, a notebook, a cobweb. Using "Footprints" as your model, examine the subject closely, commenting on its various parts; then, like Velikovsky, base an assumption on your findings.

   Or set up an unsatisfactory or oversimplified concept, make an analysis that knocks it down, and conclude with a newer and better explanation.

   Suggested concepts:
   a. The pen or printed book is mightier than the sword.
   b. This poem is "fabulous"! (Name a specific poem.)
   c. Franklin says that we dress to please others.

2. After reviewing Professor Smith's analysis of dialects in "Your Language Says More Than You Think," make a plan for a composition giving an analysis of your own. Listen closely to the conversation of someone you do not know well—a passenger on a city bus, a clerk at the book store, a voice on the radio. Analyze the vocabulary, word choice, grammar, and pronunciation so that you can arrive at logical conclusions regarding the formal education, social standing, or attitudes of the speaker.

   Or you might choose to analyze a condition or situation. Begin with a central idea and support it with your analysis.

   Suggested central ideas:
   a. Crank telephone calls are a national problem.
   b. Mentally deranged persons are walking like lions in our streets.
   c. A man's words say less than his tone of voice.

Catherine Ursillo

3. Analyze a concrete thing—such as a fragment of cloth, the skin of a banana, a peach seed, a compass, a popcorn popper, the lock on a door, an electric typewriter. Conclude your analysis with a summary statement.

4. Perhaps the picture on this page will give you ideas for a composition that analyzes some of the causes of college turmoil.

Making an Analysis   **225**

Combining various types of writing

The following four selections are examples of compositions that combine two or more types of writing: opinion, personal experience, description, definition, analysis, and so on. As you read these articles, study the various ways authors organize and develop their ideas.

The Euphemism: Telling It Like It Isn't

The Editors of Time

Modern American speech, while not always clear or correct   1
or turned with much style, is supposed to be uncommonly frank.
Witness the current explosion of four-letter words and the ex-
plicit discussion of sexual topics. In fact, gobbledygook and nice-
Nellyism still extend as far as the ear can hear. Housewives on
television may chat about their sex lives in terms that a decade
ago would have made gynecologists blush; more often than not,
these emancipated women still speak about their children's
"going to the potty." Government spokesmen talk about "rede-
ployment" of American troops; they mean withdrawal. When
sociologists refer to blacks living in slums, they are likely to
mumble about "nonwhites" in a "culturally deprived environ-

ment." The CIA may never have used the expression "to terminate with extreme prejudice" when it wanted a spy rubbed out. But in the context of a war in which "pacification of the enemy infrastructure" is the military mode of reference to blasting the Viet Cong out of a village, the phrase sounded so plausible that millions readily accepted it as accurate.

The image of a generation blessed with a swinging, liberated language is largely an illusion. Despite its swaggering sexual candor, much contemporary speech still hides behind that traditional enemy of plain talk, the euphemism. 2

From a Greek word meaning "to use words of good omen," euphemism is the substitution of a pleasant term for a blunt one—telling it like it isn't. Euphemism has probably existed since the beginning of language. As long as there have been things of which men thought the less said the better, there have been better ways of saying less. In everyday conversation the euphemism is, at worst, a necessary evil; at its best, it is a handy verbal tool to avoid making enemies needlessly, or shocking friends. Language purists and the blunt-spoken may wince when a young woman at a party coyly asks for directions to "the powder room," but to most people this kind of familiar euphemism is probably no more harmful or annoying than, say, a split infinitive. 3

On a larger scale, though, the persistent growth of euphemism in a language represents a danger to thought and action, since its fundamental intent is to deceive. As Linguist Benjamin Lee Whorf has pointed out, the structure of a given language determines, in part, how the society that speaks it views reality. If "substandard housing" makes rotting slums appear more livable or inevitable to some people, then their view of American cities has been distorted and their ability to assess the significance of poverty has been reduced. Perhaps the most chilling example of euphemism's destructive power took place in Hitler's Germany. The wholesale corruption of the language under Nazism, notes Critic George Steiner, is symbolized by the phrase *endgültige Lösung* (final solution), which "came to signify the death of 6,000,000 human beings in gas ovens." 4

No one could argue that American English is under siege from linguistic falsehood, but euphemisms today have the nagging persistence of a headache. Despite the increasing use of nudity and sexual innuendo in advertising, Madison Avenue is still the great exponent of talking to "the average person of good upbringing"—as one TV executive has euphemistically described the ordinary American—in ways that won't offend him. Although this is like fooling half the people none of the time, it 5 has produced a handsome bouquet of roses by other names. Thus there is "facial-quality tissue" that is not intended for use on faces, and "rinses" or "tints" for women who might be unsettled to think they dye their hair. In the world of deodorants, people never sweat or smell; they simply "offend." False teeth sound truer when known as "dentures."

Admen and packagers, of course, are not the only euphe- 6
mizers. Almost any way of earning a salary above the level of ditchdigging is known as a profession rather than a job. Janitors for several years have been elevated by image-conscious unions to the status of "custodians"; nowadays, a teen-age rock guitarist with three chords to his credit can class himself with Horowitz as a "recording artist." Cadillac dealers refer to autos as "pre-owned" rather than "secondhand." Government researchers concerned with old people call them "senior citizens." Ads for bank credit cards and department stores refer to "convenient terms"—meaning 18% annual interest rates payable at the convenience of the creditor.

Jargon, the sublanguage peculiar to any trade, contributes 7
to euphemism when its terms seep into general use. The stock market, for example, rarely "falls" in the words of Wall Street analysts. Instead it is discovered to be "easing" or found to have made a "technical correction" or "adjustment." As one financial writer notes: "It never seems to 'technically adjust' upward." The student New Left, which shares a taste for six-syllable words with Government bureaucracy, has concocted a collection of substitute terms for use in politics. To "liberate," in the context of campus uproars, means to capture and occupy. Four people in agreement form a "coalition." In addition to "participatory democracy," which in practice is often a description of anarchy, the university radicals have half seriously given the world "anticipatory Communism," which means to steal. The New Left, though, still has a long way to go before it can equal the euphemism-creating ability of Government officials. Who else but a Washington economist would invent the phrase "negative saver" to describe someone who spends more money than he makes?

Lexicographer Bergen Evans of Northwestern University 8
believes that euphemisms persist because "lying is an indispensable part of making life tolerable." It is virtuous, but a bit beside the point, to contend that lies are deplorable. So they are; but they cannot be moralized or legislated away, any more than euphemisms can be. Verbal miasma, when it deliberately obscures truth, is an offense to reason. But the inclination to speak of certain things in uncertain terms is a reminder that there will always be areas of life that humanity considers too

private, or too close to feelings of guilt, to speak about directly. Like stammers or tears, euphemisms will be created whenever men doubt, or fear, or do not know. The instinct is not wholly unhealthy; there is a measure of wisdom in the familiar saying that a man who calls a spade a spade is fit only to use one.

QUESTIONS

1. What opinion or central idea is stated in Paragraph 1?
2. What erroneous concept is presented in the second paragraph? What is to be the authors' argument?
3. Does the definition in Paragraph 3 follow the same basic pattern of that in "Junk"? Explain your answer.
4. How do the factual materials in Paragraph 4 support the central idea? What do the facts in Paragraphs 5, 6, and 7 prove?
5. How does the final paragraph contribute to the unity of the article?

WORD STUDY

(1) *gobbledygook* and *nice-Nellyism*, (2) its swaggering sexual *candor*, (3) Language *purists* and the blunt-spoken may *wince*, (4) use of nudity and sexual *innuendo*, (5) Verbal *miasma*.

1984

Paul Goodman

There were two main movements toward rural reconstruc-   1
tion in the early '70s. The first was the social decision to stop harassing the radical young, and rather to treat them kindly like Indians and underwrite their reservations. This humane policy —instead of raids of Treasury agents on the colleges, horrendous sentences for draft card burning, cracking children's skulls on the Sunset Strip—was the idea of social engineer Donald Michael, of the Institute for Policy Studies. Michael argued that, if the serious aim of society was to increase the GNP, it was more efficient to treat the non-conformists like Indians. Natu-

From 1984 by Paul Goodman. *Ramparts*, September 1967. Copyright © *Ramparts* Magazine, 1967. Reprinted by permission of the Editors.

rally, this was difficult when their reservations were in the middle of metropolitan areas, like the Haight-Ashbury or East Greenwich Village, or on the big university campuses. But this plan became much more feasible when an inventive tribe, the Diggers, suddenly remembered the peasant and Taoist origins of their ideology and began to forage in the country.

The second wave of ruralism was the amazing multiplication of hermits and monks who began to set up places in the depopulated areas for their meditations and services to mankind. There had always been individuals who felt that the mechanized urban areas were ugly and unhygienic and who therefore fled to the country, at first only for the summers. (I remember a nest of these in the '50s around Wardsboro, members of the Congress for Cultural Freedom supported by the CIA.) But it was not until the early '70s that humanists began to realize that society had indeed reverted to Byzantine or Late Imperial times, and who therefore withdrew to save their souls.   2

These two kinds of emigration sufficiently explain, I think, the present patchquilt of settlement in Vermont. On the one hand, where the Diggers settled, there are square-dance communes with their unauthentic mountain music and the extraordinary effort to develop a late-frost hemp, something like the inept taro culture in Micronesia. The Diggers have been called lawless, but their simple code—(1) Live and Let Live, and (2) the Golden Rule—is probably adequate for their simple lives. Except for the ceremonial hemp, their agriculture is strictly for subsistence; many of them live like pigs anyway. On the other hand, the hermits and the religious, with their synods according to Roberts' "Rules of Order" and their Finnish-style wooden architecture, perform social services by running Summerhill-type schools and rest homes for the retired. And their beautiful intensive and glasshouse farming, copied from the Dutch, provides the only tasty urban food now available. Beside these, there are the gurus like Goodman, who lives across the Connecticut and is terribly old.   3

The two distinct types coexist peaceably and of course are peaceable people. Indeed, it was during the Vietnam troubles that society first began to encourage their exodus, to get them out of the Pentagon's hair. It happened this way: Diggers and many other youths were burning draft cards in embarrassing numbers. In desperation, to get them away from settled places, the *agents provocateurs* began to schedule the be-ins and T-groups further and further out in the sticks, with transportation paid by the CIA. To the government's surprise, this caught on. The urban young suddenly decided it was groovy to dig up   4 carrots right from the ground, to shake down apples, and to fuck the sheep; they began to camp out, and then to squat and settle. They also imagined they would grow hemp. Many professors, meantime, after signing several hundred anti-war protests in the Times (for which, by some slip-up, they could *not* get a CIA subsidy), finally became conscience-stricken about working for M.I.T., Columbia and Berkeley, and quit and set up little colleges in the hills. The rest is history. But it was not until the Kennedy-Wallace administration that the official policy of land grants and rural subsidies began. (As we shall see, this was after the Seven Plagues.)

At present there is plenty of mixing between Digger types   5 and professor types, though at the beginning they hardly communicated. When some authentic music comes to Vermont from Tanzania or Cambodia, it is common to find beatniks with their matted hair and lice sprawled on a professor's maple floor; and there is intermarriage. I do not mean to imply that Diggers are unattractive. Some are unkempt in a becoming way, some are diamonds in the rough, a few are real barbaric dandies. On the whole, they are sweet and serviceable people, are glad to serve as school aides, pull weeds, etc. The professors, in turn, are democratic and would like to teach them something, but unfortunately there was the break in the cultural tradition that occurred at the time of "Don't trust anybody over 30." Since the young wouldn't trust anybody—justifiably—they couldn't learn anything. And now their own children have an unbreakable apperceptive block, impervious to Head Start programs.

Common elements in the Vermont culture are fresh food,   6 good hi-fi and much playing of musical instruments, jalopies of all vintages, disregard of moral legislation and low taxes. At some level, all are good citizens. Public services are cheap, roads are good enough, because everybody pitches in. It is touching to see Diggers who won't wash their faces carefully depositing their beer cans in litterbaskets. Another common element is, of course, Senator Aiken, who is now 100.

QUESTIONS

1. Remembering that Paul Goodman's "1984" appeared in the September, 1967, issue of *Ramparts*, comment on the point of view established not only by the title but by the reference to the early seventies. Is his approach really fanciful or factual or both? Explain your answer.

2. What classifications does Goodman present? How are they developed?
3. What is the author's purpose? Is the selection a parody? A political satire?
4. Can you find reasons for classifying sections of the article as (a) opinion, (b) analysis, (c) argument, (d) classification?

WORD STUDY

(1) to stop *harassing* the *radical* young, (2) the *Diggers*, (3) *inept taro* culture in *Micronesia*, (4) the *ceremonial* hemp, (5) the *agents provocateurs* began to schedule the *be-ins* and *T-groups*, (6) it was *groovy* to dig up carrots, (7) the *Kennedy-Wallace* administration, (8) *unkempt* in a becoming way, (9) an unbreakable *apperceptive block*, *impervious* to Head Start programs, (10) another common *element* is . . . Senator Aiken.

A Provincial in New York: Living in the Big Cave
Willie Morris

The apartment I found was in the east twenties, between   1
Madison and Park. The other places that I had seen and liked,
airy places with parks nearby, never rented for less than $250
or $300 a month, for rents in the city were criminal. This one
rented at $125, and it occupied the third floor of a narrow gray
building next to a parking lot. The exposed side was pocked
with holes and ridges, and someone had written on it in white
enamel: "The Dukes." Looking at this unusual structure from
a block down the street, one was struck by its lean-to quality;
it seemed to have no business existing at all. It rose from the
west side of the parking lot, gaunt and improvised. Someone
walking down the street with the address almost always walked
right past it, thinking that the place might not be inhabited. One
reason may have been that there was a red canopy over the sidewalk at the front door advertising the short-order take-home
service which shared the entrance off to the left.

From A PROVINCIAL IN NEW YORK: LIVING IN THE BIG CAVE, from *North Toward Home* by Willie Morris. Houghton Mifflin Company, 1967. Reprinted by permission of the publisher.

One walked up the three flights through several padlocked 2
doors, often past the garbage which the landlords had neglected
to remove for two or three days. Once inside our place, things
were not bad at all. There was a big front room with an old
floor, a little alcove for a study, and to the back a short corridor
opening up into a tiny bedroom for my son and a larger bedroom in the back. The kitchen was in the back bedroom. I had
not been able to find a view of an extensive body of water at
popular prices, but from the back window, about forty yards out,
there *was* a vista of a big tank, part of some manufacturing
installation in the building under it, and the tank constantly
bubbled with some unidentified greenish substance. From this
window one could also see the tarred rooftops of the surrounding
buildings, and off to the right a quiet stretch of God's earth, this
being the parking lot next door.

From the front room the view of the street was more ani- 3
mated. Across the street there was a large bar which seemed
to remain open twenty-four hours a day, and in front of this, on
the corner, one could look down at any hour and see the little
circles of people, just standing, watching the mad traffic on lower
Madison. We were without sunlight, which was unable to penetrate down from the tall office building across the street; and
when it rained, which was often that first year, I remembered
the hard cold rainfalls in the Mississippi delta of my childhood,
and how they encompassed the green earth and fields and trees
in such a torrent that one seemed at the mercy of nature itself;
here, from the front window, the rain merely kicked up little
pools of dirt and debris on East 26th, and sent people under the
canopy of the bar. One oppressive Saturday afternoon, our old
Texas friends Ronnie Dugger and Larry Goodwyn sat here in
our front room with us; our separate work had all brought us
briefly together in New York City. We sat here talking of old
times and places; then, out of a gray sky, there came a blizzard.
We watched the big flakes come down for a while, a little de-
pressed and intimidated. Suddenly Goodwyn opened the window, stuck his head out, and gazed down at the scene on East
26th. Then he put his head back in, turned around, and said,
"Well, boys, they got us all up here together . . . and then they
snowed on us." The subway was also difficult to get used to.
There was a station twenty yards from the building; every five
minutes the building rocked and groaned at its very foundations.

I was only seven blocks from my office at *Harper's*, and in 4
the mornings I could walk up Madison to work. On a fine day,
carrying my black briefcase with poems from housewives in the
Midwest, or stream-of-consciousness prose from the graduate

schools, I enjoyed making my way up the avenue through the bustling crowds on the sidewalks, feeling very much the cosmopolite. But on some grim foggy morning, when the steam came out of the sewers in the streets as if the earth beneath were on fire, the city had a dreadful claustrophobic quality, like death itself: closed-in, blind, and airless, compressed by the endless concrete and asphalt exteriors. The horns from the cabs, the cursing of the drivers, the harsh violence of the streetworkers dodging the already clogged traffic, caused a new arrival to feel that humanity here was always at war with its machines and with itself. In the course of a year, walking seven blocks to work and back over the same route, I saw three people killed by cars and four others badly hurt. The most likely place for this mayhem was the curious intersection of Park and 33rd. Here there was a tunnel which came suddenly out of nowhere. Cars whipped out of it at terrific speeds, catching pedestrians crossing against the red light on Park. There was no sign suggesting the existence of this tunnel, which added somewhat to the spirit of adventure. At first it would be disrupting to see the white sheet covering an unfortunate pedestrian caught by surprise by some taxicab coming out of the tunnel, the crowds milling around with that sullen big-city curiosity looking at the blood, the cop or two waiting perfunctorily for the ambulance to arrive. After a time I grew used to the spectacle, however, and would walk gingerly past the broken body and its spectators as if it were all in the morning's walk.

Many times, walking home from work, I would see some 5 unknowing soul venture across that intersection against the light and then freeze in horror when he saw the cars ripping out of the tunnel toward him. For a brief instant the immobile human would stand there, transfixed by the vehicle bearing down upon him, the contrast of desperate vulnerable flesh and hard chrome never failing to send a horrible tremor through an onlooker's being. Then, suddenly, the human reflex would take over, and the pedestrian would jackknife first one way, then another, arms flaying the empty air, and often the car would literally *skim* the man, brushing by him so close it would touch his coat or his tie. If another car coming behind did not nail him then, much the way a linebacker moves in for the kill after the tackle or end merely slows down a ball-carrier, the pedestrian would stand there briefly, all the blood drained from his face, oblivious to the curses from the driver of the car which had just missed him. If there was a cop on the corner he would wait while the man staggered in his shock to the sidewalk beyond, there to accost him: "Ya crazy, hah? Ya stupid? Walkin' against the light!

Hah! Ya almost got killed, ya know it? Ya *know* it?" I saw this ritual several times; on one occasion, feeling sorry for the person who had brushed against the speeding car, I hurried across the intersection after him to cheer him up a little. Catching up with him down by 32nd I said, "That was good legwork, sir. Excellent moves for a big man!" but the man looked at me with an empty expression in his eyes, and then moved away mechanically and trancelike, heading for the nearest bar.

On a number of occasions on my peregrinations from 33rd to 26th there would be some bum sprawled out on the sidewalk, and the people would walk right past him, or sometimes step over him, glancing back a little nervously, usually saying to their companions, "Somebody should call a cop." The first time I saw a man lying prone on the concrete, blood trickling slightly from his nose, I bent over and asked him if he was all right, and he moaned a little, and I went into a restaurant and phoned the police to report his distress. But after a while, like the others when confronted with such a sight, I would keep going too, though always a little guiltily, wishing a cop would come by soon. Why should people in such a city be *expected* to stop and do something about their fallen wounded, not knowing them nor caring? The existence involved in moving daily to and from work in the immense and faceless crowds inevitably hardens one's senses to violence and despair. I came to feel it perfectly natural, this isolated callousness of the city-dweller. Anyone who expected valor or compassion in everyday acts in a monstrous American city in these times expected too much of human nature, and would sooner or later be disappointed. The cops became the guardians of benevolence; they were our salaried Samaritans.

6

QUESTIONS

1. How many various types of writing does Willie Morris combine? Point out passages to illustrate each type.
2. What comparisons or contrasts does the author use? Do these support an opinion, enliven description, clarify a personal experience?

WORD STUDY

(1) gray building . . . gaunt and *improvised*, (2) *stream-of-consciousness* prose, (3) of desperate *vulnerable* flesh, (4) arms *flaying* the empty air, (5) on my *peregrinations* from 33rd to 26th.

A Devout Meditation in Memory of Adolf Eichmann

Thomas Merton

One of the most disturbing facts that came out in the Eich- 1
mann trial was that a psychiatrist examined him and pronounced
him *perfectly sane*. I do not doubt it at all, and that is precisely
why I find it disturbing.

If all the Nazis had been psychotics, as some of their leaders 2
probably were, their appalling cruelty would have been in some
sense easier to understand. It is much worse to consider this
calm, "well-balanced," unperturbed official conscientiously
going about his desk work, his administrative job which happened to be the supervision of mass murder. He was thoughtful,
orderly, unimaginative. He had a profound respect for system,
for law and order. He was obedient, loyal, a faithful officer of a
great state. He served his government very well.

He was not bothered much by guilt. I have not heard that 3
he developed any psychosomatic illnesses. Apparently he slept
well. He had a good appetite, or so it seems. True, when he
visited Auschwitz, the Camp Commandant, Hoess, in a spirit
of sly deviltry, tried to tease the big boss and scare him with
some of the sights. Eichmann was disturbed, yes. He was disturbed. Even Himmler had been disturbed, and had gone weak
at the knees. Perhaps, in the same way, the general manager of
a big steel mill might be disturbed if an accident took place
while he happened to be somewhere in the plant. But of course
what happened at Auschwitz was not an accident: just the routine unpleasantness of the daily task. One must shoulder the
burden of daily monotonous work for the Fatherland. Yes, one
must suffer discomfort and even nausea from unpleasant sights
and sounds. It all comes under the heading of duty, self-sacrifice,
and obedience. Eichmann was devoted to duty, and proud of
his job.

The sanity of Eichmann is disturbing. We equate sanity 4
with a sense of justice, with humaneness, with prudence, with
the capacity to love and understand other people. We rely on
the sane people of the world to preserve it from barbarism, mad-

ness, destruction. And now it begins to dawn on us that it is precisely the *sane* ones who are the most dangerous.

It is the sane ones, the well-adapted ones, who can without qualms and without nausea aim the missiles and press the buttons that will initiate the great festival of destruction that they, *the sane ones*, have prepared. What makes us so sure, after all, that the danger comes from a psychotic getting into a position to fire the first shot in a nuclear war? Psychotics will be suspect. No one suspects the sane, and the sane ones will have *perfectly good reasons*, logical, well-adjusted reasons, for firing the shot. They will be obeying sane orders that have come sanely down the chain of command. And because of their sanity they will have no qualms at all. When the missiles take off, then, *it will be no mistake.* 5

We can no longer assume that because a man is "sane" he is therefore in his "right mind." The whole concept of sanity in a society where spiritual values have lost their meaning is itself meaningless. A man can be "sane" in the limited sense that he is not impeded by his disordered emotions from acting in a cool, orderly manner, according to the needs and dictates of the social situation in which he finds himself. He can be perfectly "adjusted." God knows, perhaps such people can be perfectly adjusted even in hell itself. 6

And so I ask myself: what is the meaning of a concept of sanity that excludes love, considers it irrelevant, and destroys our capacity to love other human beings, to respond to their needs and their sufferings, to recognize them also as persons, to apprehend their pain as one's own? Evidently this is not necessary for "sanity" at all. It is a religious notion, a spiritual notion, a Christian notion. What business have we to equate "sanity" with "Christianity"? None at all, obviously. The worst error is to imagine that a Christian must try to be "sane" like everybody else, that we *belong* in our kind of *society*. That we must be "realistic" about it. We must develop a *sane* Christianity: and there have been plenty of sane Christians in the past. Torture is nothing new, is it? We ought to be able to rationalize a little brainwashing, and genocide, and find a place for nuclear war, or at least for napalm bombs, in our moral theology. Certainly some of us are doing our best along those lines already. There are hopes! Even Christians can shake off their sentimental prejudices about charity, and become sane like Eichmann. They can even cling to a certain set of Christian formulas, and fit them into a Totalist Ideology. Let them talk about justice, charity, 7

love, and the rest. These words have not stopped some sane
men from acting very sanely and cleverly in the past . . .

No, Eichmann was sane. The generals and fighters on both   8
sides, in World War II, the ones who carried out the total destruction of entire cities, these were the sane ones. Those who have
invented and developed atomic bombs, thermonuclear bombs,
missiles; who have planned the strategy of the next war; who
have evaluated the various possibilities of using bacterial and
chemical agents: these are not the crazy people, they are the
sane people. The ones who coolly estimate how many millions
of victims can be considered expendable in a nuclear war, I pre-
sume they do all right with the Rorschach ink blots too. On the
other hand, you will probably find that pacifists and the ban-
the-bomb people are, quite seriously, just as we read in *Time*,
a little crazy.

I am beginning to realize that "sanity" is no longer a value   9
or an end in itself. The "sanity" of modern man is about as useful
to him as the huge bulk and muscles of the dinosaur. If he were
a little less sane, a little more doubtful, a little more aware of his
absurdities and contradictions, perhaps there might be a pos-
sibility of his survival. But if he is sane, too sane . . . perhaps we
must say that in a society like ours the worst insanity is to be
totally without anxiety, totally "sane."

QUESTIONS

1. How does Thomas Merton's "Devout Meditation" differ from
   other types of expository writing? What is the principle of organization or arrangement of details?
2. What is the author's opinion of Adolf Eichmann? How does
   Merton analyze Eichmann's behavior?
3. How does Merton define sanity?
4. How persuasive is the author as he argues with himself? Explain your answer by pointing out relevant passages.
5. Is the final paragraph indirect persuasion or strong summary?

WORD STUDY

(1) If all the Nazis had been *psychotics*, (2) calm, "well-balanced,"
unperturbed official, (3) any *psychosomatic* illnesses, (4) to *rationalize . . . genocide*, (5) into a *Totalist Ideology*.

Michael Keller

SUGGESTIONS FOR WRITING

1. Take time to meditate on the future as you look at the photograph on page 240; then write a composition developing your main ideas. Or meditate on whoever or whatever interests you, such as Che, the Beatles, Thomas More, ghosts, reincarnation, death, immortality, a flight through space. Use as a model Thomas Merton's "A Devout Meditation in Memory of Adolf Eichmann."

2. Write a composition based on one of the following titles or on a similar title of your own. For your model choose either "The Euphemism: Telling It Like It Isn't" or the selection from "A Provincial in New York."

   Suggested titles:
   a. The Myth: Telling It Like It Wasn't (*or* Was)
   b. The Stock Market: An Economic Thermometer
   c. A New Yorker in the American Desert
   d. A Californian in a Foreign Country

3. Write your own version of 1984. Either present your views as prophecies, or use the flashback approach as Paul Goodman does in "1984." Before doing this assignment, you may wish to read or reread George Orwell's *1984* and compare his style with that of Paul Goodman.

A 0
B 1
C 2
D 3
E 4
F 5
G 6
H 7
I 8
J 9